A LIFE IN SII

BY GERALD COUNTER

Published by: Jules P. King

9 Barrington Mead, Sidmouth, Devon, EX10 8QW

To Vera, Susan and Olwen

Acknowledgements

I have long wanted to write my life story to leave to my family, but I couldn't have done any of it without all the characters I have met throughout my 86 years.

One of these characters is Julian King, a close friend, whom I first met back in July 2010 by the ford over the river Sid. He came up to me and asked if I was Gerald Counter. He told me he was researching the land just across the river, where his house now stands, on what was once Merrifield Meadow and was also interested in the old water mill and iron foundry, and asked me if I would like to help him and I told him I would.

Our first get-together was in the afternoon of Wednesday 1 August 2010 when we walked through the old foundry site and around where the mill once stood.

We met again on Monday 20th September 2010 at Julian's house and this was the beginning of regular Monday afternoon sessions, where we discussed local history and drank 'green' tea till it came out of our ears!

We both enjoyed our get-togethers and these lasted right through the next 28 months, until I was diagnosed with MND in January 2013.

So, to Julian who is helping me finish what I started and to everyone I have ever known, because they are the people that made my life what it is, thank you.

Gerald Counter

Table of Contents

Preface

Gerald and I met and became friends through a common interest in local history. We enjoyed each others company such that no subject was taboo and no secrets remained hidden. Gerald had previously shown me the first chapters of his autobiography, so I knew it was something he wanted to complete and leave to his wife and children.

In January 2013, when he was finally diagnosed with MND and his muscles deteriorated to such an extent that he could no longer write or use his computer, I suggested that I help him finish what he had started. The first session was on 6 February shortly after Gerald and Vera moved into Room 121 at Holmesley Nursing Home in Fortescue, Sidmouth. What followed was many sessions were I took notes about his life in Sidmouth. We finished the draft version of the book on Wednesday 12 June at the Royal Devon & Exeter Hospital (Wonford), the day before he passed away.

Often, during our sessions, and mainly to stop me getting writers cramp, Gerald and I put the book to one side and had other sessions where we would do Q & A's about all manner of things from bee-keeping to the supernatural, from literature to 'What If?' We enjoyed many hours of conversation doing this and amazingly found many things to laugh about. Anyone who knows Gerald will know he has a wicked sense of humour.

We also spent many hours editing my errors from previous sessions. You have to remember that Gerald is a true Devonian and I am a foreigner from London. This meant, at times I had no idea what Gerald was on about and this continued to be a source of amusement between us. It took me about 4 weeks once, to discover that it wasn't 'Coronation' he was talking about, it was 'chlorination,' and I've never understood why 'Mousehole' is pronounced 'mowsall' and Fowey is pronounced 'foy,' but as I said, I'm a foreigner from London!

I'm telling you this now so that if you find any errors in the book you can rest assured they are mine and not Gerald's!

It is also common knowledge throughout Sidmouth that Gerald did indeed know everybody and everything about the town and was never short of a story or two, or three, or four.........!

I just want to reassure anyone who reads Gerald's story that although I was involved in writing it, this is his story in his own words, told as only Gerald could tell it.

So, put your feet up, relax, and get to know a truly remarkable man, a man who was kind, passionate and humble, and who respected all regardless of position or background with equal measure.

To be in his presence was to know how to life your life.

Julian King

Foreword

I had it in my mind during my working years to leave a record of my life for my family but it wasn't until 2010 that I actually sat down at the computer and started writing it.

I was born in Sidmouth on the 25 April 1927 and have lived here all my life, and this is a true record of my life in the town, a town I've always loved and never wanted to move away from.

One of the big changes throughout my life has been the physical change in the community. Today, you very rarely really know your next door neighbour. In the old days, if my mother was ill, Mrs Previs would come across and keep an eye on her. If my mother went out to Exeter shopping, I'd go to Mrs Previs and she'd look after me till she got back. But that community's gone, because today there are so many holiday cottages instead of old fishermen. But then that's inevitable, because things change and move on and something that stays still decays and rots. But I've always liked my town and I was quite chuffed to be told by the two National Judges, whom I met at the National Honey Show one year, that Sidmouth was the cleanest seaside place in England and that we had one of the most respected Town Clerks in the country.

I've always liked my town and never wanted to go anywhere else but I was lucky, I ended up with a decent job which I enjoyed. I mean, I went to every household in the town. I met all sorts of people from all classes and I always took the view that if I only learnt one new word a week for my vocabulary, I'd gained something in life.

I don't think I've squandered my life at all. There are things I haven't done that I would have liked to have done, like play rugby and join the armed forces to broaden my mind more. Vera always says I'm 'narrow,' I'm not wide enough in my thoughts, but I'm interested in most things and you mustn't look back in life. If you look back too much you can get depressed.

I never wanted to move or go anywhere else and neither has Vera. She never wanted to go back to Wales. She fell in love with Sidmouth when she came here in 1946 and she has always been proud of her town, like me.

I've led a full life and enjoyed every minute and I wouldn't have changed my life or my style of living for anything. I've led a simple life, near to nature and my grass roots. My mother was a Sidmouthian from an old Sidmouth fishing family and I was brought up in a happy family environment.

I have three sisters but of the four of us I was the only one who stayed in Sidmouth. Rene went to Dartford, Rosie went to Liverpool and Margaret went to Wellington in Somerset. I was the only one who stayed with my grass roots.

What more could I ask for? People pay £600 a week to come here on holiday. I've lived here all the time! I hope all that read this book will enjoy my life story, as much as I have enjoyed living it.

Gerald Counter

A Life in Sidmouth

Chapter One: The Early Years

The Early Years

A Life in Sidmouth

I arrived in this world on Monday 25 April 1927. My mother told me it was a lovely spring day. I was the last of four children born to Ernest and Edith Counter, three sisters had preceded me. Seven years before my arrival there were twin girls, Irene May (Rene) and Rosina Elizabeth (Rosie), and, seven years before the twins, my eldest sister Margaret Ellen was born. It was what today we would call a well-planned family.

My mother, Edith Maude Counter, came from a Sidmouth family of local fishermen by the name of Harris, and my father, Ernest Thomas Counter, came from the village of Kenton a few miles southwest of Exeter. He came to the town seeking employment and his first job was as a gardener, at Willoughby House on Peak Hill. He obtained lodgings with a Mr & Mrs Gosling, who lived in cottages opposite. These belonged to Mr Truman who had a tea shack at the top of the hill.

A pal of my father introduced him to my mother. My mother who was five years younger, used to work in what is now the Hotel Riviera, but in those days was three private houses. She also used to work in Cannister House, opposite 'The Old Mason Arms' pub in Chapel Street. This was a private house owned and occupied by a family called McCloud. I understand from my mother, that part of the building was used as a private laundry. I remember the old gaunt three-storey building well. It was demolished in the 1960s and it stood where, Western Court now stands.

My mother lived with her parents, Robert and Rosina Harris (née Franks), in Coastguard Cottages in York Street with her two sisters and older brother. My mother and father were married in 1909, in the Sidmouth Parish Church, by the Reverend Clements. They started their married life in Western town in a small terrace house in Silver Terrace. Western Town is an area behind the Hotel Riviera and Bedford Hotel. Many of the fishing families lived in this part of town in those days, which is often referred, to as Bedford Square. Most of these properties were pulled down in later years and replaced by flats.

The Early Years

My mother could remember Stephen Reynolds, the doctor's son who came and lived with the Woolley family. He came to Sidmouth because of poor health. He lived here for many years and during that time wrote several books on life in the fishing community.

Western Town in the late 1890s to early 1900s used to suffer serious flooding from heavy seas during winter gales. Water used to pour down what was known locally as 'The Gut' which was the gap between the Bedford Hotel and the Hotel Riviera. This, I understand was a regular occurrence in those days.

After my eldest sister Margaret was born, my parents left Silver Terrace in Western Town, and went to live in the old School House in Mill Street and became caretakers of the Parish Hall. The cottage consisted of two bedrooms, a front room and living room, a scullery and an inside toilet. There was no bathroom. Lighting was by candle or oil lamps. The rent, 5/- a week according to the rent book, which I have now donated to the Sidmouth Museum, was paid at £2-5s-0d every nine weeks.

This was the old Boy's School until about 1912 when it became the Parish Hall and was owned by The Sidmouth Educational Trust and was administered by Sidmouth Consolidated Charities. The Parish Hall was the social centre for the town and it continued as such until about 1947 when it became Auction Rooms for Messrs Potbury's, and, as such until about 1982.

When my parents moved to the old School House, they became responsible for letting, cleaning, and preparing the Parish Hall for functions, setting out tables and chairs, and cleaning up afterwards.

The hall was used for all sorts of functions. On Saturday nights dances were held between 7.30pm and 11.45pm. My mother used to provide refreshments; tea, coffee, and various sandwiches and cakes. Tea and coffee was 3d, sandwiches and cakes 4d. The dances always stopped by 11.45pm due to it being Sunday next day.

I used to help my mother at times. I always remember that when every one was gone, we would lock up and when we came outside in the street, under the street lamp at the bottom of Holmdale, there was always a local Policemen there to see all was well.

He would say, 'Everything all right Mrs Counter?'

My mother would always ask him into the Cottage and give him a hot drink and sandwich or cake. However, whatever the weather you could guarantee a Constable would be there!

I can still remember some of the bands that played there; Percy Hill and his group, Norman Huck and his band and Ernie Dommett's Band.

Weddings receptions were held there too and my mother would help to prepare and organise things. In 1939, with the war looming, the hall was used for many different purposes. The Ministry of Labour used it, as a recruitment office. The gentleman in charge was Colonel Ward. The Parish Hall later became a school again, bringing it back to its original purpose.

At the start of the 1939-45 war, Sidmouth received about 500 evacuees from the Stoke Newington area of London. They came with their Headmaster Mr Wall, his wife and some of their teachers, and local families took them in.

Their education, and ours, still had to continue, so a system was set up where they came to our schools. We had to adapt, so we went to school in the mornings one week, and the following week afternoons, and vice-versa.

Some of the older boys in the top class, known as 'Standard Seven', used to go to a hut in Water Lane where we had to learn how to repair some of the evacuees' shoes. This was something new to us but we had in our class the son of a shoe repairer named Mortimore. The business spanned three generations. Mervyn Mortimore was able to instruct us to a certain level. It only goes to say, we were far from perfect, but after a few weeks, the work was passable.

Most of the evacuee children came from poor backgrounds and from a very different environment but after a time they blended in and adapted to our ways. It must have been terrible to be uprooted from your family and sent to a completely unknown place amongst complete strangers. All they had were a few personnel belongings, and only their teachers and school friends. What was this place called Sidmouth and the people here like? It must have been very upsetting for them, but they soon adapted to our ways, they played our games and friendships developed over time.

My earliest recollections in life are being taken to be weighed at a clinic which was in or near Woolcombe House. I can remember other babies and children being there. The person who weighed me was a Mrs Dingwall whose husband was assistant to Mr R. W. Samson the well known local architect. Most of the house's built in Bickwell Valley that can be seen to-day, built before the 1939-45 war, were his design and built by W. J. Skinner. Mr Samson left us with some lovely buildings the likes of which we will never see built again in this valley.

As I write this, a planning application has been approved and the Fortfield Hotel will be pulled down and replaced by some luxury flats. To me the developers have already created a monster of a building next door that is totally out of keeping with Sidmouth, and the properties are selling at prices from £500,000 to £750,000.

Chapter Two: School Days

School Days

A Life in Sidmouth

I have digressed a little, so to return to my early days. Being the only boy and the youngest I was made a fuss of by the rest of the family.

My first weeks at school must have been terrible for my mother. I remember to this day her taking me, holding my hand walking up Holmdale, along the High Street to All Saints School, taking me into the classroom and handing me over to the teacher.

She kissed me good bye and said, 'I will come and collect you at dinner time!'

We were put where we had to sit by our teacher, Miss Purchase, who was a lovely person. However, after a time I decided that I did not want to stay and ran out of the school and all the way home, but my mother took me back to school. I had to go, whether I liked it or not.

This tantrum went on for a week or more. A lady who lived at 9 All Saints Road gave me a penny bar of chocolate one day to placate me, but I ate it and ran home again. Eventually I settled down.

The school was a Church School attached to All Saints Church. The Vicar was The Reverend Keith Steele. We always went to church on Ascensions Days and just before Christmas.

Every year before Christmas there was a bazaar in the church hall. One thing that I always remember about the bazaar was that there was a bran tub just inside the entrance of the hall. This consisted of an open-ended barrel, which contained small cork granules amongst which small gifts were hidden. We children paid two pence and had to put our hand in the tub and pull out a gift. This we thought was great fun! The money raised was given to church charities, which helped the poor in Africa.

Besides our teacher in Class One, there were two sisters, Misses Nancy and Dolly Keel, who took Classes Two and Three. Class Four was Miss Golf and the top class was taken by Miss Partridge, who was also the Head Mistress. It was a very happy school and you were there until you were ten years old.

There were children from two families who had to walk approx two to three miles to get to the school as there were no buses then in their area. Barbara and Kenny Burnell walked in from Fortescue and Eddie Beer and his sister walked in from the village of Salcombe Regis. I do not remember them ever being late for assembly or missing school. In winter they would arrive wet or cold, and they brought their own sandwiches as there were no school dinners in those days!

All the children that went to All Saints School were local. We knew each other and all our parents were born in the Sidmouth locality.

On reaching ten years of age, you left All Saints School and went to Senior School in Vicarage Road. You started here in Standard Four and finished in Standard Seven by which time you were fourteen years old and you left to go out into the world of work.

At Senior School, we learnt woodwork and gardening. On Thursday afternoons Mr Jasper took Standard Four for football, Mr Jim Mills took Rugby in Standard Five. Our football field was known as Vicarage Field, which was just behind what is now Culver House, Victoria Road and Glebelands. This was the original vicarage before it was sold and became a private guest house. The new vicarage was in Manor Road, next to the present car park opposite the Westcliffe Hotel. When we played rugby, we had to march down to the rugby field next to Sidmouth Hospital.

Our class was about thirty-two in numbers. Our day started with assembly, a prayer, a hymn and any notices were read out. This all lasted about twenty minutes. After assembly we went back to our various classrooms for lessons which started with religious instructions, which again lasted approximately twenty minutes. This was followed by mental arithmetic then mathematics which lasted until playtime.

A Life in Sidmouth

Playtime lasted for fifteen minutes, during which we drank our milk. Every one was allowed milk in glass bottles which contained ⅓ of a pint for which two pence a week was collected, on Monday mornings, by your class teacher.

For the older boys, one morning, there were Woodwork lessons. Our teacher, who taught us carpentry, was Mr Wilf Mills. He was a brother to teacher Jim Mills mentioned above. The girls had domestic science, in other words cookery lessons.

Usually when the girls had cookery we boys had gardening classes. There were twelve plots with two pupils to each plot .and we grew all sorts of vegetables. We would dig and prepare the ground in the autumn. Trenches were made for peas, beans etc. and the soil was prepared according to what seeds were to be sown.

One incident I well remember; Mr Mills told me and my plot colleague to prepare a trench, 4ft wide and the length of the plot for a row of onions.

I mentioned this to my father, being a gardener, and he said 'What a load of rot!'

The next week when we were on our plot, I said to our teacher, 'My father said this is a load of rot!'

I was sent to the headmaster for insubordination plus four strokes of the cane!

Once a week we had keep fit. There were music lessons and I was hopeless. Our music teacher was Mr Rodgers who lived in Seaton and was an organist at a local church. He was very much a disciplinarian. He was a bachelor and lived with his parents. He was the first teacher to be called up. He went to Egypt and was killed. I wrote his parents a letter of sympathy and I had a lovely reply from them. For many years I sent and received a Christmas card from them until they passed away.

School Days

Our curriculum consisted of English Grammar, Reading lessons, Geography, History, Science, Mental Arithmetic and Poetry.

I was never in love with school, but when I look back, it was a happy period of my life. We use to get up to all sorts of pranks. On one occasion I received ten strokes with the cane when I had brought a quantity of pepper to school and blew it around the class causing every one to sneeze! When Christmas came, they produced a satirical play about me.

In one science lesson, we brought seawater in to do an experiment to show that if the water was boiled it left a salt deposit. In the middle of the experiment myself and Mervyn Mortimer turned off the main gas-tap to the Bunsen burners. Needless to say we were sent to Mr Giles the Headmaster where we received the cane!

On another occasion, one of the boys in our class had forgotten to bring his lunch, so we persuaded him to run home to fetch it and told him the quickest way home for him was to go over the Mill Stream that ran round the bottom of the school grounds. He went to jump the Mill Stream but he fell in the middle and was soaking wet, so there was more trouble.

At the start of the War we were all issued with a gas-mask in case of a gas attack, which never came. Where Fulfords Estate Agents is, at the time of writing, this was the distribution centre. The gas-mask was in a brown box about 8" square with a string to carry it over one's shoulder. The mask was made of rubber with a cellophane window and a filter, with adjustable straps to fit it on one's head, and we had to carry them where ever we went.

When there was any danger a siren would sound giving a loud high pitch noise. For an alarm it sounded three times, but when the danger was passed it gave out a continuous sound for the 'all-clear.'

When we were in school, we used to leave our class rooms and go into some nearby trees and bushes when the siren sounded, and stay there until the 'all-clear' sounded.

A Life in Sidmouth

After awhile, if the alarm went off, it was arranged that if we lived near by or had a friend who lived nearby, you could go to their house. I had a friendly classmate, Mervyn Mortimore, who's grandparents lived quite near, so I use to go to their house at 4 Lawn Vista when an alarm sounded, and return to school when the 'all-clear' sounded.

On the whole, school was a happy period of my life, and now when I look back, I regret I never used the opportunities that were available. I suppose when you are young, one's mind and thoughts are on more immediate things. But one thing that I remember at school was that the Headmaster and one of our teachers used to keep a couple of hives of bees under an apple tree. Some of us boys use to watch them open the hives and handle the bees.

This always fascinated me and may have had some influence on my later life, as you will find out further in this book.

School Days

Chapter Three: Growing Up in Sidmouth

Growing Up in Sidmouth

A Life in Sidmouth

When I look back, growing up in Sidmouth was great, but my parents were strict and my mother's word was 'law.' My father was much more easy going, but we were brought up to respect others, to behave and be polite to our elders. In school we were always being told that 'manners make'th man!' If you met your teacher outside school you touched your cap or forelock. This was just being courteous. Our family was a happy one.

My father was very hard working. I always remember him being the gardener at Cotmaton House in Cotmaton Road, now Abbeyfield House.

In 1935 Mr Tyndall who owned Cotmaton House moved to Mannor Road. Cotmaton House was put up for sale and was eventually purchased by The Reverend Cannon Elsey who had retired from Liverpool Cathedral. When he came to live here he brought all his domestic staff with him but my father continued to be employed there as gardener until the owners widow sold it in about 1960. When it was sold, and became a hotel, my father left. He had worked there for about thirty years and in those days he worked Monday to Saturday but Saturdays only till one o'clock.

Next door was another big house called Cotmaton Hall. For many years my father used to work in the garden there on Wednesday afternoons. On Saturday evenings between 6pm and 7.30pm he used to go there and tend to whatever needed doing in the greenhouses, and during the winter months my father would go there on a Sunday morning and fill the fires up with coal or coke.

The lady who owned Cotmaton Hall, a Miss Winch, only lived there for a few weeks each year. The rest of the year she lived in Switzerland. It was a lovely old house.

In 1935, Cotmaton Hall was sold to a local syndicate of developers who were going to turn it into flats. But early one November morning, I think about 6am, the police came to get my father to say that the house was burning down. When he got there the fire engine was damping things down. The house was nearly destroyed and it was never rebuilt.

On Saturday afternoons in spring and summer he would spend his time working at his allotment up on Salcombe Hill. As a small child I used to go with him but I expect I was more of hindrance than a help. One thing I remember, when he planted his potatoes he would load up his wheel barrow with his seed potatoes, sit me on top and push me all the way up to the 'plat.' The plots were always referred to as 'plats.'

There were about seventy allotments on Salcombe Hill, forty above Alma Lane, and about thirty on the left hand side, opposite the junction of Salcombe Hill with Alma Lane. Most of these were rented by local fishermen or builders. The rents were 2/6 a year. The plots were well cultivated and the main source of vegetables for families in those days.

On Good Fridays most of the holders would be seen working on their plots. It was the first holiday of the year and they brought a snack and I can remember flagons of Cider being passed around. I still remember some of their names; Curly Langmead, Lew Bartlett, Jockey Harris, Tom White, George 'Gibric' Bastin, Richard 'Grundy' Soloman and Taggie Salter.

Taggie Salter was a real character and was excellent at using a scythe. At one time in the early 1930's he had a smallholding at the bottom of Redwood Road when it was a field. 'Taggie' used to go jobbing-gardening and he always smoked a pipe and wore an old cap. If he had a flower in his cap, it meant he had work, but if there was no flower he was available to take on some. He also used to keep a few pigs during the WWII.

One Sunday morning I went across to his plot which was on the other side of the road to ours. This was about 7am, and Taggie had slaughtered one of his pigs on the quiet. There he was with a couple of mates with buckets of scalding water scrubbing and cleaning the carcass. During the war one had to apply for a licence. I assumed this was being 'done on the qt.' Good luck to him I thought, that pork tasted better because of the circumstances and the way it was produced.

A Life in Sidmouth

In those days there was a sprit of community and every one knew each other. Although times were harder, people helped each other and there was a sense of belonging. When a neighbour was ill others would turn to help. People pulled together. When my mother was ill our neighbour swept the front and cleaned the brass on the front door.

What's happened today? We have lost our responsibility to each other, we are strangers to one another. People are much better off, we are more affluent, but it comes at a price? The problem with affluence is people don't know how to use it. I could see it coming. My job used to take me into every home in the community. I began to find that more mothers were going out to work and children came home to an empty house to do what they pleased. Up till 1945 we lived in closer communities and we all knew each other. Since the end of the war, there has been a great social and economic shift.

I am not condemning this, and one has to be careful not to generalise, but today we live in a more material world, which has caused us to lose the 'social-glue' which held us together. People are more mobile today. We knew all the neighbours and every one in the street passed the time of day. If someone was ill, you enquired. We were a close knit community and everybody helped one another. We children ran errands for people to the shops.

After school we would hurry home to tea, playing games on the way home. After tea it was down to the beach, swimming in the summer, fishing over the river. We used to go down to 'Red Wall' just below The Ham weir catching eel's There would be about half a dozen of us seeing who would catch the biggest and the most.

We used to make 'feather-boats.' At the back of the Anchor Inn in Old Fore Street, Back Street to us locals, Belle Vue Dairy had a shed where two men were employed plucking and dressing poultry. We used to go and ask for feathers to fit into our boats; wing feathers were best. Then we used to go to the boating pond down on The Ham and sail them. We even had races with them. This was around 1936. It was a lovely boating pond with two small fountains at each end. It was quite popular. There would be some boys with motor boats and proper yachts.

At the end of Millford Road a Mr Pitt lived. He worked for Fields as a cabinet maker etc. He came here from the Isle of Wight after the First World War. He hand made three of us boys a lovely yacht each to sail on the pond. All the rigging and sails were made by him, and also a stand for the boat to sit in when not in use. He was a real craftsman and if the boats got stranded on the fountains we would wade in to free them.

In the summer months we would spend all day down on the beach and we would take our dinner and tea down there. We used to spend hours swimming and prawning on Chit Rocks and Lade Foot.

I got into awful trouble once with my Mum. I wanted some 'setting-nets.' Setting-nets are larger than 'skimming-nets' which are about 10" across on a long handle and used to 'skim' along the sand under the rock ledges, but my mother got Uncle Bill Harris to make me a single skimming-net, instead of 4 setting-nets that I really wanted. I was very disappointed, about it.

Anyway, one day when I came home from school, my mother, who was a member of Mothers Union had gone to their monthly meeting. We had very long lace curtains in our front room. I went and got the sewing scissors out of the sewing-box and cut a 'yard' off the bottom of each of the lace and tied the pieces onto two wire hoops I had made, and that was my setting-nets! Alec Baker and me went off and tried them out near Chit Rocks one day after school. There wasn't much of a tide but we caught a few prawns.

In the meantime, my mother found out what I had done. She gave me a good hiding and sent me to bed. Then, every day for a fortnight, once I got home from school I had to go straight to my bedroom. As I have said my mother was very strict and if you misbehaved that was her punishment.

A Life in Sidmouth

After a while I got bored in my bedroom so I tried to find things to amuse myself. I had a wind-up gramophone and played old 78 records like Charles Penrose singing 'The Laughing Policeman' or I read books and comics.

I also found my trusty old water-pistol in the bedroom but I had no water. As I said previously, we didn't have a bathroom and I wasn't allowed downstairs. I used to 'wee' in the potty under my bed so I decided to fill my water pistol with the contents of my potty! I then sat cross-legged on the window sill in my bedroom, which was about two foot thick, and squirted my water pistol at people as they passed by below without them seeing me!

I remember another occasion when one of my twin sisters had left home and gone out to work in domestic service, which most girls did in those days as that was the main source of employment. Anyway, my sister, on her day off, had been to Exeter and bought a new dress.

Where we lived in the old School House, which is now Counters Court, we had a small garden at the rear of the premises which was accessed via a gate from what was once the playground. Between the rear of the Parish Hall and this garden was a yard that housed some toilets and a water tap. My mother used to hang out her washing in the garden.

On this occasion my mother sent my sister to bring in the washing, I was in the yard playing with a hosepipe and when she got inside the gate I squirted the water all over her. The dress shrank and she couldn't wear it. There was no sanforized material in those days! I was given the cane by my mother and again was sent straight to bed from school for a week!

When I look back we all had our various jobs to do. On Saturdays my sisters had to clean the cutlery and clean their shoes. My father used to give us tuppence to clean his boots ready for when he went to rugby on Saturdays.

Like all children we would fall out at times but on the whole we soon made it up. We always went to Church on a Sunday morning and Sunday School for an hour in the afternoon. When I got older it was Bible Class at Church House from 2pm till 3pm.

My sisters being 7yrs older than me had to go out into the world of work when they left school at 14yrs. They went into domestic service, although the twins had both done little jobs on a Saturday for a few hours.

My sister Rosie used to help a Mrs Hawkins do her shopping and by helping her she taught Rosie dressmaking skills that were a great help to her.

Her Sister Irene used to help at a sweet shop in Fore Street called Freeths where Boots the Chemist is now. It was a lovely shop. It also sold ice cream in the summer months. Irene only used to do a few hours on a Saturday. The full time staff were Elsie Woolley and Rene Mortimore. I can remember going in with my mum and sitting down at a table which had reddish brown tiles with oak edging and having an ice cream wafer served in a glass dish.

In those days Freeths was about the only place to buy ice cream, except for a chap on a three wheel bicycle with a box on the front selling 'Walls' ice cream, lollies and 'snow-fruits' at 1d or 2d each.

During the summer months there were two ice cream carts one by the entrance to the promenade opposite the York Hotel, and one by the Bedford Steps entrance. One was owned by Mr Smith, the other by Mr Parrott, who also owned a fish and chip shop in York Street. All the ice cream was home-made, 1d cornets or 2d for a wafer. The carts were nicely painted with a sign written in bright cream and yellow paint. The owners always wore white coats with an apron tied around their front and a white trilby hat.

You will wonder how it was kept cool but the cylinders of ice cream were surrounded by ice that came from Selleys Ice Works. I wonder how many can remember the old ice works in behind

Knights and Bennett & Rogers? It was known as Selleys Yard back then. About 5pm you would see the errand boys who worked at the fish shops and any shop or hotel that needed ice would all descend on Selleys Ice Works to collect the blocks of ice ,which were about 2ft x1ft 6ins by 4ins thick.

Back then we had four fish shops, J Hooks, Mocks, MacFisheries and Bert and Lucy Daveys. J Hooks was next to Holland & Barrett, Mocks was where Stead & Simpsons are now, MacFisheries was where Taste is now, and Bert and Lucy Daveys is now the 'Silver King' Chinese Restaurant at the top of Newtown opposite All Saints Road.

We lads that went Prawning went to the fish shops for our bait to tie in our nets. We would take an old bucket and ask for the remains, mostly of old plaice, which had been filleted. They would stink. John Mortimore and I always also had a couple of stale kippers that we tied into our nets to attract the Pawns. Sometimes we would sell our catches to Daveys to get a bit of pocket money. He was very fair we used to get 2/6d a dozen for the large prawns.

Prawning was usually done at night. We would go on a new or full moon when the tides are at their longest. When you went one would dress up in old clothes and always wore heavy boots with hobnails on the bottoms which enable you to get a grip on the rocks which were slippery. Remember this was at night-time; we would leave home at 10pm and return home again about 3am in the early morning!

We would leave home after baiting our nets when the tide was just beginning to fall. By the time we had walked down to Lade Foot the tide was right to fish. Prawning means wading out to the rocks to drop your nets down under the ledges to catch the prawns as they go out with the tide. You set the nets for about 10 minutes then pull them up, hoping you got some prawns or may be a Lobster in the net.

Sometimes there would be many people down there, and names that come flooding back to me are Peter Weeks, Norman Charles,

Harry Stevens, Harry Pike, Ken and Stan French and Ted Searle. But in my mind the best one of all was the late Harvey Culverwell. John Mortimore and I went with Harvey, for many years, from about 1946 to 1980, and we had some great catches. However, Harvey always had the most, and to us he was a legend!

Today no one goes at night, not many by day, perhaps only John Mortimore and Terry Horn. The Prawns don't seem to be there. I must admit after the very severe winter of 1962-3 it was never quite as good. But looking back it was a good time to be around. It is sad that no one has carried on these old traditions.

Chapter Four: Activities

Activities

A Life in Sidmouth

There were many other pleasurable things we used to enjoy doing. In the autumn we would go getting chestnuts, and in the spring we would go up Salcombe Hill to what was known as Tadpole Pond with a jam jar to collect tadpole spawn or get some newts. We also used to get up at 4am, walk the fields under Muttersmoor which look over the Otter Valley, or go to the top of Trow Hill and pick Mushrooms, and be home in time for school, or work when we were older. During the last war we would go off at 4am and be back by 7:30am with a basket full. John Mortimore used to go with old Charlie Stone the Cobbler. They would walk up Salcombe Regis to Manyards to gather the mushrooms, but again this tradition has died out.

The quantity of life has improved but the qualities gone. The early morning is the best part of the day. The air is fresh and crisp and the light gives a clearness like no other time of the day.

There were various things we used to go to. I well remember going to 'Coral League.' This was held at the rear of Dr Grant Wilson's residence which was where Woolworth's was, now M & Co., on Tuesday nights from 6pm till 7pm. We made things with plywood and other wood using a fret saw. These articles were sold at sales of work and the funds went to support Missionaries in Africa.

We always had to go in by the rear entrance, which was in Russell Street. A Miss Bolton used to run 'Coral League.' She was a relation of Robert Bolton the sweet pea specialist in Essex. The two pillars which are now the rear entrance to M & Co. were where the rear entrance was. Two large wooden doors about 8ft high and the right hand one had a little door cut in it. The front of the house had a small pebbled forecourt and an attractive chain linked to white post. The front door was green with a brass knocker. A letter box which was kept beautifully polished as was their name plate.

On Wednesday nights there was the 'Church Lads Brigade' run by Mr Leonard Fry and Jim Martin in the Parish Hall. They would teach various drills and rifle-shooting and they also had their own band, and about twice a year they would parade around the town.

There was also keep-fit and exercises using parallel bars and a vaulting horse. I think there were about thirty to forty members.

Also on Wednesday nights there was the 'Girls Friendly Society.' This was a club run for girls who could meet together one night a week to listen to a talk or just a chat and they had a choir. Their first location was a room in the upstairs of the Old Market, but when it was demolished in the 1930s they moved to Heydons Hall which is now part of the Sidmouth International School. My mother and a friend Emma Bastin use to run it. They used to provide a hot drink, tea or coffee, cocoa and biscuits. Cocoa was more popular in those days.

I think the reason for this club was to give young girls somewhere to go one evening a week. There was some connection I think with the Parish Church. Some of the ladies behind the club were prominent members of the church. One lady I remember was a Miss Fielding who lived at Brinkburn in Manor Road, and a lady known as Sister Cooper. She wore a grey uniform with the Church Army embroiled on the lapels. She came from Droitwich and was involved in moral and social work. The 'Girls Friendly Society' produced a play once a year.

The club existed for about 25yrs until the out break of WWII, when most of the girls were called up or went into factories, to take up war work. This was also the end of young girls leaving school and going into domestic service full time.

Another Society was 'The Band of Hope.' It met on a Thursday night between 6pm and 7pm in the Parish Hall and was primarily for young people, to tell them about the evils of drink. There would be a talk and some games and hymns would be sung.

Once a year 'The Band of Hope' would have an outing to Harpford Woods. It was a half day outing in the old 'Toast-Rack' which would take us out and bring us home. While out in the woods we would have sports with different races and a tug-of-war, the winners received a 2d bar of Nestles chocolate. Mr Searle, known to every one as Tom, his wife and her sister, lived in a cottage which went with his job, and was situated in a clearing in the wood. Mr Searle who was the Forrester for Clinton Devon Estates had erected some swings, see-saws, tables and benches where you could have a picnic.

If you didn't bring your own food you could purchase various things from Mrs Searle at the Cottage. Freshly made tea was always available made from water from their well. At week ends in the summer months there would be quite a few people out there.

There were plenty of walks in the woods and places to explore. The railway line between Sidmouth and Sidmouth Junction ran through the woods and under the track was a Tunnel which linked the woods either side of the track. We children liked to walk through the tunnel and shout at the top of our voices and it would echo all though the woods.

Another annual outing was the 'Sunday School' day trip to Exmouth. We would be up early, have breakfast, get ready, and then go over to the 'Three Corner Plot' or 'Triangle' as it is now known, to get the coach. The younger children were accompanied by their mothers. Most of the children took packed sandwiches with them which we ate on the beach. Exmouth has a sandy beach, and if you didn't watch out you would end up with sand in your sandwiches and your mouth! The sand on Exmouth is very fine and when dry the least bit of wind will blow it all about.

We would leave the Triangle about 10am and return about 6pm, tired but happy, after having a lovely time, weather permitting.

If the weather was good most of our summer holidays were spent down on the beach, providing Mum didn't want me to run any errands. We would be off first thing in the morning, taking what food we were given, and, there we stayed mucking around over Chit Rocks, swimming on and off, and getting sun burnt playing cricket on the sand at Jacobs Ladder.

Activities

We taught ourselves to swim by going into the sea and doing what was known as the dogs-paddle. Then we would gradually improve our strokes. There were always a few of us together. I remember on several occasions going out in a rowing boat with a Mr Tommy Hazelock, jumping in the sea with our clothes on, and swimming around for some time. Tommy would go home. We would swim in to the beach, lie in the sun, and dry ourselves. We boys mostly whore khaki shorts and shirts which soon dried in the sun.

We used to go on the rocks out to 'Crabs Hospital,' which was the furthest south lying rocks about twenty yards beyond Chit Rocks down below the Clockhouse Restauarnt at Connaught Gardens. There we would lift rocks searching for crabs or lobsters, and then we would call in at cricket field on the way home to have a knock about.

I remember once I caught a lobster which was about 18" long and 3" thick across his back. It must have been a real old one because it had white barnacles all over it. As I picked it up and threw it against the rocks my pipe fell out of my mouth and extinguished itself in the sea. I remember selling the old lobster for £3 to Pard Bellamy who worked in 'Hookway' bookmakers (later 'Whites' Bookmakers) at the back of John Mortimore's shoe shop.

One thing we always did was to go to the waste bins, which were situated just outside the entrances to the promenade opposite Clifton Cottage and the Bedford and York Hotels. The bins in those days were tall and made like wire baskets. We would ferret through them to find empty cigarette packets for cigarette cards which we used to collect. Back in those days most boys collected them. There were different ones, always 50 in a set, and you could get an album to stick them in. The sets consisted of various interests, like Wild Flowers, Cricketers, Football Stars, Kings and Queens of England, Wild Birds, Dogs, Fishes, and many others.

In those days there were no take away food establishments so the cigarette packets were always clean. There was always a trade in cigarette cards taking place, what was known as 'swapping.' If you had two of one card you swapped it with someone who had what you wanted to complete your set. 20 Kensatis cigarette packets had Flags of The World which were made in silk. The complete sets of cards in mint condition today can fetch quite a sum of money at an auction or dealers.

Another thing that was popular with the boys was comics and magazines which cost 2d. There was a different one published every day;

Monday was the Adventure

Tuesday the Rover

Thursday the Wizard, and

Friday was the Champion, Boys Cinema and the Hotspur

These weekly comics and magazines contained several different stories in each issue. Ones that come to mind are 'Rockfist Rogan R. A. F.' and 'Colwyn Dane Detective' in the Champion. After you had read yours you would swap it with someone else for one you didn't have, and in that way you got to read them all.

I think it was through these comics and magazines that we were encouraged to read and expand our interest in books generally, and eventually one ended up joining the library. It got me interested in books on the Incas and Aztecs. I have never regretted reading for it has increased my knowledge and understanding of what's going on. It opens up whole new fields of interest, nature the arts, politics.

One unusual incident I remember from my childhood happened when I went with my mother and her sister Eva to see a pantomime at the Manor Pavillion. I remember I went to a show with my mother and my sister and we were sat there and the show had been going about half an hour. There was Mary Schofield, whose mother had a shop at the top of Newtown, now Sue Ryder Care charity shop, and the production was 'Ali Baba & the Forty Thieves,' and I can see it now, they had these big pots on the stage, and whether it was children or grownups, came up when the show started and appeared out of these pots.

Anyway, Mary Schofield had this show on, it was in 1937, it had been going about half an hour, and all of a sudden the curtains came across, the lights came on, and Mary Schofield appeared on the front of the stage and asked if Colonel and Mrs Archer was in the audience because Salcombe Hill House was on fire? This was their residence, which later became known as Salcombe Hill House Hotel. Colonel and Mrs Archer were sat well down in front of us, and I remember them getting up. They must have had a party with them, because they used to do that years ago, didn't they, and they all trooped out, then the show recommenced.

It was a bad fire and they couldn't return there to live. It was later bought by someone else, and the architect R W Sampson was involved in it, and it was re-opened as a hotel. Mr Rory Blake, who worked for Potbury's, became Managing Director, and it was him and his wife that ran it as a hotel. In the summer they had a sale up there of damaged goods, and Colonel Archer was a model railway enthusiast, and up in the attic, I mean it was big place up there, and I remember going up there and seeing all this charred wood and that, and Dick's (Dick Longhurst) father bought an engine and some railway track in the sale. They were down here while the sale was on and they went up there because Dick had a model railway.

Chapter Five: Hard Times

Hard Times

A Life in Sidmouth

My mother's cousins were fishing people and in the summer they would run fishing trips for mackerel in the bay and also trips to Ladram Bay which cost 2/6d or a trip to Beer for 7/6d. Sometimes we would get a free ride or be allowed to steer the boat with the tiller.

As I write this, I can still hear the old fishermen shout, 'Trip in the bay', or 'two hours mackerel fishing, keep what you catch.'

This money would help their income as it was hard times in the twenties and thirties. Although their income and living standards were very poor they were very proud and independent men and women. They were a very close-knit community who stood together in good times and bad and nothing was wasted. Clothes were handed down to younger brothers and sisters and my mother used to have my trousers re-seated by a tailor named Mr Marks.

I remember on one occasion my mother had acquired a rain coat, from somewhere and she got Mr Marks to alter it to fit me. I can remember going to have fittings done at his house which was at the bottom of Peaslands Road. Anyway, this coat, which to me was an awful light beige colour, must have belonged to a lady because the button holes were on the right. Mr Marks made a lovely job of the alterations but after I found out it had been a ladies coat I wouldn't wear it!

When I look back, my mother was very hard working and resourceful. She used to take in washing, and my sisters had to go and fetch it on Monday mornings before going to school. Later, when I became older, I had to collect it. There was one lot from a house in Bickwell Valley and another lot from from a house on Salcombe Hill.

The lot from Salcombe Hill was always the most, and always in a washing basket tied down with a blue checked cloth. The lot from Bickwell Valley was always in a small attaché case.

When I took the washing back they would pay me. My mother put a bill inside. I never knew how much she got until one day I saw the amount my mother charged. All she got was 2/3d in old money. She charged 3d for vests, 3d for knickers, 4d for petticoats, 1d for stockings and 6d for jumpers and blouses. I use to hate Mondays because it was washday.

Also on Mondays, after my mother had finished her washing she would go across the yard to the Feoffees. This was a large gaunt house, which was home to eight old women who had been in domestic service in private houses and become too old to work. They had to look after themselves.

The house consisted of a ground floor in which resided a couple who were like caretakers. The two floors above had a long corridor with six rooms, three on either side, the two centre rooms on either side were known as workrooms, and at the far end of the corridor on each floor was their toilet. The two rooms each end were where the residents lived. There was a fireplace and a bed in the rooms, a table, a chair and perhaps an armchair and other personal belongings which they brought with them when they moved in.

They usually stayed there until the end of their days .I think they were supplied with a hundredweight of coal per week, most of the time. Today we would say they were living in poverty.

My mother used to give one of these old ladies a roast dinner on Sunday. Her name was Lizzie Smith. She had worked for Major Cony in Convent Road. Lizzy used to tell me things if I took her something my mother had made her. I used to ask her what she had for breakfast and she told me she always had 'Kettle Broth.' I wondered for years what this was so one day I asked her! It seems this was her breakfast most mornings. I was shocked when she told me it was bread with hot tea poured over it. I just couldn't believe it.

She used to say, 'If I can afford it I might be able to have a little milk in it.'

I have never forgotten Lizzy Smith. She was a dear old soul.

A Life in Sidmouth

I still remember some of the other ladies surnames. They were Dunn, Arscott, Mitchell, Bolt, Maeer, Skinner and Barge. They just lived, ate and slept in their rooms.

The two centre rooms on each landing were known as the work rooms. Here they would do their cooking on an old gas stove. Their washing was also hung up to dry in this room and there was a galvanised coal bunker in which their weekly allowance was kept. There were no baths at this time, 1938, just a sink to wash themselves and prepare their meals.

They did their own cleaning, except for the workroom floors and landings and stairs of which there were thirty eight in all. These were scrubbed every Monday by my mother after she had finished her washing. In our Cottage we had an old fashioned 'Copper' which my father would fill with water and light up on Monday morning for my mother before he left for work. In the afternoon, after she had finished her washing and after her dinner, she would carry buckets of hot water to do the scrubbing in the Feoffees. It took about 3hrs. She had two shillings for this, which went toward our rent.

My father always came home to dinner, so on Monday he would help my mother put the sheets etc. through a large cast iron mangle that we had. He would turn this great big wheel and I can remember my mother putting a blue bag in the tub. The blue bag made the whites whiter. Then she would make up some 'Robins' starch for the collars etc. Then when all that was done, there was the ironing to finish!

My mother always seemed to be working to me, no pleasures like we have to day. There was no washing machines or spin dryers. It was damn hard work, but I never heard her ever complain.

Hard Times

A Life in Sidmouth

Chapter Six: Christmas

Christmas

A Life in Sidmouth

My mother was a first class cook and we always had good home cooked food. She made the most delicious veal and ham pies and her apple cake was out of this world. We always had good food and never went hungry and there was always a wide variety of good wholesome food on the table.

In those days chicken was a luxury. My father always kept a few chickens so we always had fresh eggs. When they had finished their laying-span he would kill them and we had them over several weeks for Sunday roast. They always seemed to taste so much nicer than poultry to day.

At Christmas we always had roast goose and a piece of pork with all the trimmings.

My mother always made her Christmas puddings and mincemeat several weeks before Christmas. We all took it in turns to stir the puddings and make a wish at the same time. The Christmas cake was cooked, then the marzipan was made and the cake was eventually iced.

Christmas Eve was always a busy day. The Mince Pies had to be made and she always made a large trifle in a willow patterned bowl. It consisted of sponge fingers in the base then fruit with jelly, then a layer of custard and finally finished with desiccated coconut and dotted with glace cherries. About a half a cup of sherry was added, and it was served with fresh clotted cream.

In those days we used to pop to the dairy at the end of the road or go up Holmdale to Mrs Maeer for 6d worth of cream in a dish. There would be about ½lb of lovely cream that was made fresh each day.

Christmas was a wonderful time. We would wake up early to see if Father Christmas had been.

Mother would say, 'Go back to sleep, he hasn't been yet!' but we would look to see if our pillowcase, had anything inside.

Christmas

There where no sophisticated toys like today. There was usually a tin of 'Blue Bird' toffees, some chocolates and some books. I once had a little train set and a second hand toy car with real lights which were powered by a battery.

I believe it was given to my mother by a Miss Violet Elton who lived in Beatlands Road. She was a lovely person. I believe she learned to play badminton in India when she was a little girl, and later, when she came to England, she joined a club near her home in Kensington and started playing in tournaments. This was before WWI. Between 1920 and 1930 she won the All England Ladies Doubles championship on five occasions and represented England. She liked to play tennis in the summer. Violet Elton retired to Sidmouth and died here on 4 March 1969.

Although my mother was a wonderful cook, my father always cooked the Christmas dinner, which was followed by Christmas pudding and then mince pies all served with clotted cream. When we had the Christmas pudding there were always three-penny pieces inside for luck. These were put in when the puddings were made.

Our sideboard had nuts and dates, oranges and apples and the house was always decorated with holly, mistletoe and paper chains which we made at school.

One thing that springs to mind was, that about a week before Christmas some of the children in our street would be invited each year to go to a house called Woodbine Cottage in Millford Road which was owned by a Mrs Kent and her daughter Madeline. They lived there for many years and each year we were invited to go there and have a glass of lemonade and a fancy cake and a small gift for Christmas.

We went for many years until they moved to a cottage in All Saints Road. The children who lived in Mill Street were always invited, the Webster children went along and my sisters and I would go for about an hour. Mrs Kent would ask how we liked school and about how we were getting on there.

A Life in Sidmouth

In the weeks before Christmas my mother used to dress up in a Father Christmas outfit. She would go around to different houses in nearby streets where there were children and knock on the doors and ask the children what they wanted for Christmas. She did this up until she died in 1942. When the evacuees came Mr Chaloner borrowed the suit for a Christmas party for the evacuees and never returned it. My mother had made the outfit herself. She was good with a needle and made most of her dresses and skirts and household things like curtains, cushions etc. and dresses for my sisters when they where of school age. My mother made them on her hand-powered 'Singer' sewing machine.

Also on Mondays, after she had finished her washing and scrubbing in the Feoffees, or Alms Houses as they were called back then, my mother would change into her other clothes and go to Church House in Coburg Road to pay what was called the 'Coal Club' and 'Clothing Club.'

These were run by a Miss Cowan, who lived with her brother in St Kilda, a house in Laskeys Lane, that is now flats. There was also a single woman living there with them, who always wore a sort of nurse's outfit and went by the name of 'Nurse.' She was a companion to Miss Cowan. Working people paid into these Clubs what they could afford each week, and, when they wanted to buy clothes or coal in the winter, they would draw out the money. In a way they were like saving clubs.

On Mondays 'Nurse' would bring down Magazines for the old women in the Alms Houses, like back copies of 'The Tatler' and 'Country Life' etc. She would open our back door and leave them on a cupboard, for my mother to give to the old women. This occurred every Monday about one o'clock without fail. We would hear her open the door put the books down, and then close the door. On this Monday we heard the door open and shut and a noise, and my mother said, 'It must be 'Nurse' with the books.' She went to look, just as the door closed. There were no books. The following day Miss Cowan brought the Magazines and to say that 'Nurse' had died on Monday at one o'clock?

Christmas

Is there a supernatural? I will return to this subject later, I have other tales to relate.

A Life in Sidmouth

The Old School House
Gerald's family home at 16 Mill Street, Sidmouth
Image ©Gerald M Counter

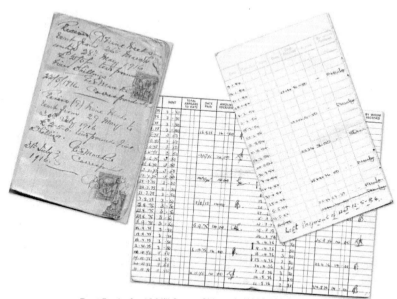

Rent Books for 16 Mill Street, Sidmouth (1916-1984)
Image ©Gerald M Counter

Gerald's Family (c.1927)
Back Row L-R: Dad - Gerald (in dad's arms)
- sister Margaret - Mum.
Front Row L-R: Twin sisters Rene and Rosie.
Photo taken outside the Feoffees building
next to family home at 16 Mill Street, Sidmouth
Image ©Gerald M Counter

Gerald's Family II
Back row L-R: Dad - sister Margaret - Mum.
Middle Row L-R: Twin sisters Rene and Rosie.
Front row: Gerald (aged about 5-6 years).
Photo taken outside back door to family home
at 16 Mill Street, Sidmouth
Image ©Gerald M Counter

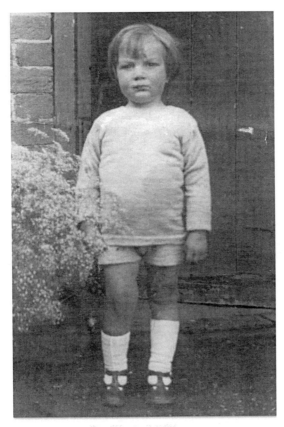

Gerald aged abt 3 years
Photo taken outside back door at
family home at 16 Mill Street, Sidmouth
Image ©Gerald M Counter

'Butter wouldn't melt in his mouth'
Gerald Aged 12
Image ©Gerald M Counter

A Life in Sidmouth

Gerald's father (Ernest Counter) at Cotmaton House
in Cotmaton Road Sidmouth (now Abbeyfield) c.1935
Cotmaton House owned by philenthropists Mr & Mrs Tindall
Image ©Gerald M Counter

Herring Fishing at Sidmouth c.1935-6
Rear L-R: nk - Woolley - 'Chip' Woolley - Tom Woolley (on far right).
Front L-R: nk - Dick Hemmett
Image ©Gerald M Counter

The Ham Rovers 1947
Back row L-R: Gerald Counter, Chris Andrews, Peter Morton, Les Cody,Peter Norman,
Frank Symington, John Southcott, John Andrews, Edward Churchill.
Front row L-R: Maurice Jones - Brian Winter - Graham Hook - David Trim
Image ©Gerald M Counter

Vera Sheppard
Taken in Treherbert in 1942 (during WWII)
when Vera was a nurse
Image ©Gerald M Counter

Gerald at Skinners Farm in Sidmouth c.1948
Image ©Gerald M Counter

Gerald and Vera on their Wedding Day 19 Feb 1949
in Vera's hometown of Treherbert.
Photograph taken at Pentre
Image ©Gerald M Counter

Vera and Gerald in Dartford
On their honeymoon in 1949
Image ©Gerald M Counter

Chapter Seven: My Father

My Father

A Life in Sidmouth

My father was always the first one up in the morning. Summer or winter, he always rose about 6am, then washed and shaved before making himself a cup of tea. He never ever had breakfast, but when he made his first cup of tea he always cracked a fresh egg into it, stirred it up and drank it straight down. He did this all his life. My father died when he was 86yrs old and he worked 3 days a week until he was 81yrs old. I can never remember him being ill until his last 6 months.

My wife thought the world of my dad; she was wonderful with him and him with her. In later years, during his illness, she used to bath and feed him. He was only ill for a short period of six weeks, the last two in hospital. My wife visited him every afternoon. Every evening my daughters and I would go to visit him and then we all came home together after visiting time was over.

My father was very fond of his granddaughters and they thought the world of him. On Saturdays they would all go out to coffee together, and at Christmas, he always took them to see Father Christmas and he would like to buy little treats for them.

On Friday nights he always went for a drink and to pay what was known as the 'Didlem Club.' It was a sort of savings club for Christmas, which was paid into throughout the year, then drawn out before Christmas. On Friday nights, my daughters were allowed to stay up a little later until he came home, when he always produced a small bar of chocolate for each of them.

At holiday times he always came with us if we went to Exmouth or some place. My father was very fond of children and one or two people from his home village, Kenton, told me that he would always take children out. I learnt later that his mother was the local Midwife in the village.

He had started out as a garden boy when he left school at 12yrs of age from his village school in Kenton. He became the garden boy for General Studd who lived at Oxen House, a large estate near Kenton and he was employed there until he left home to come to Sidmouth. He used to tell me a story about his time at Oxen House.

My Father

They had a cook there that used to like her drink. She would get my father, who was only a boy, to bring her bottles of gin from the local pub. It seems that on several occasions she was found worst for drink by her employer. He tackled my father about this and asked him if he was getting drink for the cook to which my father said he had. My father was told not to bring any more drink into the house for the cook and my father agreed. The cook was told of this.

After a couple of days the cook asked my father to bring her some gin again. My father told her what General Studd had said to him, not to bring any more drink into the house for her. She asked my father to get some and to leave it in the shrubbery outside the back door and she would pick it up. She said if the General asked him if he was bringing drink into the house he could say no, he wouldn't be telling a lie as he was leaving it in the shrubbery which was out side. This went on for a few weeks.

He was asked one morning by the General if he had brought any more drink in for the cook and my father said, 'No sir!'

Apparently they had found the cook dead on her bedroom floor that morning.

His first employment after arriving in Sidmouth was a job as Gardener at Willoughby House on Peak Hill. He was working there when he met my mother. How long they were courting for before they were married I have no idea. He was there for several years and when he left his employer gave him a reference, which was beautifully written in what we would call copper-plate writing. It said he was a most conscientious worker, polite and punctilious in his work.

He left his job at Willoughby to take up a gardening position at Sidmouth Manor. There were, I understand, several garden staff under the head gardener, a man by the name of Henry Wheaton. My father was there for about three years before leaving of his own accord.

A Life in Sidmouth

It appears one morning my father was working in the kitchen garden and his employer Colonel Balfour came along. My father said good morning to him. The next day, Henry Wheaton sent for my father to inform him that the Colonel was very displeased with him as he never said sir to him the previous day, and if this happened again he would have to go. On the Friday my father gave in his notice, so as not to give them chance to sack him.

This came to light when I was about to leave school and was at first going to go and learn gardening, and there was a job at The Sidmouth Manor as a garden boy to start.

When I came home to tell my parents my father said, 'Tell the Headmaster no, that my father had worked there for two years, and that was one year and eleven months too long!'

So I never went gardening. Instead I became an apprentice plumber to a firm in Temple Street named 'F T Dunn.' They had an ironmongers shop in the front with the workshops at the rear. The premises are now occupied by a micro printing firm called 'Hugh Simmons' at the time of writing this.

My Father

Chapter Eight: Out to Work

Out To Work

A Life in Sidmouth

Before I went to learn my trade as a plumber I had done a couple of little jobs before and after school.

My first job, in 1938, was on a Saturday morning for about 2hrs. It was delivering the local weekly paper, 'The Sidmouth Herald,' which at that time was owned and printed by the Culverwell family. The premises are now occupied on the corner of East Street by Martin McColl newsagents.

The family lived above the shop and at the rear were the printing press and a manual machine for producing posters. The machine which printed the Sidmouth Herald was operated by a gas engine with a leather belt on a large pulley and fly wheel which drove the machinery. The paper was 'put-to-bed', as they say in printing terms, on Friday afternoons.

The machinery was very primitive. At times the leather belt would break, then it was panic, and Mortimore's the shoe repairers would have to repair it post-haste. I cannot ever remember the paper, failing to appear on Saturday mornings.

I used to get 3/6d a week for delivering the paper.

Another job I got later in 1938 was delivering milk for Mr and Mrs Harris who had a dairy and a shop at the end of Mill Street by the Ford called Sid Dairy.

Mr Harris had a small farm just above Cleavedon in Sid Road which was accessed up Milltown Lane. The small holding was about forty acres in all with a couple of farm buildings, a milking parlour, and a herd of approximately twenty cows. This job came about because I was always up in the morning playing outside with a ball or over the river trying to catch a trout.

One morning Mr Harris asked me would I like to deliver milk for him before I went to school, and I said, 'I will ask my mother.'

My mother said that it would be alright, so later I went round to tell him I would take the job.

The round was a few houses in Holmdale, Millford Road, Millford Avenue, two in Salcombe Road, and three in Salcombe Hill. I carried the milk in what was called milk-crates, and, at that time milk was delivered in bottles in ½ pint, pint 1½ pint or quart (2 pints) sizes.

It took me about an hour to do the round for which I received the sum of 2/6d a week. My mother would have 1/6d of it and I had a shilling. After a while I had a bigger round so they gave me 3/6d. I had 1/6d and my mother had two shillings. I enjoyed the job and continued with this for about three years.

I liked the Harris's. They were easy going, but Mrs Harris (Beatrice) was the worker. Her husband (Walter) was on the tired side, and had a weakness for gambling. It was always said he spent two men's fortune an owed money to dealers and had gambling debts. She told me he had never been to bed, but always slept in the arm chair down stairs. He was a very tall person and I can only remember him always dressed in a tweed jacket and light Fustian breeches, heavy brown boots and a trilby hat. He looked every bit a farmer.

Mr and Mrs Harris had two children a son Martin and a daughter Betty who was the eldest by three years. Martin went into the Royal Navy at the beginning of WWII. One morning Mrs Harris received a notice from the admiralty to report that Martin was missing. It really affected her! She seemed to lose her sense of purpose and interest in things. After a time she used to chat to me about him and I got the feeling I was filling his place. Several months passed and she heard no more about him.

Then one afternoon I was on my way home from school and she was waiting at the door of the dairy shop. She beckoned me over, she was so excited. She had received a telegram from the Admiralty to say he had been rescued and was safe, and in a military hospital. She was overjoyed. She gave me the telegram to read, she was over the moon with happiness, it brought tears to me to see her so happy and elated. I ran home to tell my mother the news. The whole street was so pleased with her good news.

Unfortunately, her joy was short lived. A few weeks later she received another telegram to say Martin had died on active service. It was devastating to say the least. She never got over her loss, and became a different person. She lived for a few years but I'm convinced it affected her in mind and body.

The business was eventually closed down and the shop premises were let to Mr Coldrick's green grocers directly opposite, and used for storage. Walter Harris lived until 1962 when he died on the last day of that year. I went to his funeral, and was the only person there apart from his daughter Betty and her husband. It was bitterly cold and the ground was covered by about one foot of snow. His grave is to the south of the Chapel in the part of the cemetery that looks across the valley to his small farm in Sid Road. This was the beginning of one of the coldest winters for many years, and lasted for about eight weeks.

Looking back, at one time in Mill Street we had several shops. There was a garage, a cobbler, a barber, two fruit shops and small grocers.

At one time the Co-Op had a large store there with a bakery at the rear. This building was where the Mill Street Crafts shop now stands. On the right hand side was the grocery department and on the left was the boot and shoe dept which also sold haberdashery, curtains and furnishings. About twelve people were employed there, including the Bakery.

On Christmas morning local families would take their turkeys, geese and Christmas joints to the bakery for roasting. The men would come in specially to cook them. The charge was 6d each roasting tin. You took them to the bakery at about 9:30am and then collected them about 12:30pm.

Out To Work

My next job was as an errand boy for Mr Elkins. He owned a high class shoe shop in the Market Place next to Gliddons the Ironmongers. I worked there from April 1939 until I left school in July 1941. Mr Elkins was a single man. He lived with his mother above the shop.

During term times I went there straight from school. I would go to a room behind the shop where Mr Elkins had some tropical fish tanks, and there would be a cream cake or doughnut and a glass of milk or orange juice waiting for me before I started work.

I had an errand-boys bike for delivering the customers purchases. In pre-war days most things were delivered to the gentry. The practice was for customers to call at the shop and request some new shoes which were sent out to them on 'appro' (approval). I would take up to eight pairs of shoes for the customers to try on in their home over several days, and then bring back those they decided not to have.

My first job each evening would entail taking all the shoes and boots that customers had brought to the shop during the day for repair, to one of two local repair workshops, either Mortimores in East Street or Mr A Sparks in Temple Street. These shoe repairers were first class craftsmen. Foot wear in those days was of top quality, all made of leather. The better class men's shoes were long soled and hand sewn.

I would then bring back the repairs I had taken the previous day. These were sorted and placed in strong brown bags an addressed for me to deliver. Also any new shoes that had been purchased during the day I would deliver.

Many a time I have watched the different cobblers make the hole in the welt and new leather sole with a tool called an 'awl,' and pull through the waxed thread as tight as possible. They wore a leather guard over the thumb and palm of their hands for protection to stop the waxed tread from cutting into the skin.

A Life in Sidmouth

On Saturdays I would start at 9am. First I had to sweep the front of the shop, clean the windows and wash all the paint work. After that was finished I would go in the kitchen and prepare any vegetables for Mrs Elkins to make lunch. I would sit and have a drink of some sort before I started delivering any new shoes that had been purchased or repairs.

Before I left Elkins on Saturdays I always had to take a small box of groceries to an old couple who lived in 64 Arcot Park. I think the old lady was Mrs Elkins sister. Also on Saturdays, at about 4pm, I would go to Santers the grocers, which was then opposite Gliddons, and I would fetch one dozen tins of Mock Turtle Soup. Next I went to Mrs Coates in Church Street and got two fifty boxes of Players cigarettes. This was a ritual every Saturday before leaving.

It was a lovely place to work and I was treated with kindness and respect both by Mr Elkins and his mother, and also the other member of staff, Miss Rita Selway who had been there for many years. She was employed there until she was called up for the Women's Royal Air Force during the war.

Our customers were mostly well to do people who lived in the large houses in the area. One customer I remember was Mr Alister Fox who came to live here during the early part of the war at Rock Cottage, Peak Hill. Whenever I delivered anything there I was always given a small tin of Foxs Glacier Mints. I believe he was the managing director of the firm.

The shop only sold high quality shoes, namely Norvic, Clarks, K's, Churches Arch-Mould, Delta and Lotus. Plastic which is used today in shoes was unheard of before the war and shoes were nearly all made in Great Britain. Today, because of the economics of cost etc. most of our shoes are made abroad because of cheaper labour cost, transport, and other factors at work. The firm of Loakes, which still make good quality shoes, cuts out all the various parts of their shoes, send them out to Taiwan to be assembled and then sent back to this country all ready to be sold.

I enjoyed working at the shop; Mr Elkins was a good employer. During holidays I would start at 9am each morning by cleaning the windows and washing the front of the shop down, and then I would take out any deliveries.

During the summer when things were quiet Mr Elkins would say, 'It's quiet Gerald, there's a good tide, you can go down prawning but look in about 4pm to see if we need you.'

I stayed with him until I left school and I went into the building trade to become an apprentice plumber. On the Saturday I left Mr Elkins employment, his mother called me to her flat, to thank me for all I had done for her, during the time I had worked there.

She gave me an envelope and said 'Here is something to buy some tools with, but don't tell my son Earnest, then he will have something for you!'

That evening when I finished Mr Elkins also gave me a envelope and a reference for my new employer. When I got home my mother opened the envelopes and inside each of them was £10 with a letter thanking me for all I had done. On Monday I went down to thank them both.

All the time I was employed there I was paid 7/6d per week during term time, and 15/6d during holidays. In those days it was good pay, and one of the better paid errand boy's jobs in the town.

Back then most shops had an errand boy to deliver their goods. To name a few there was Zoogal Salter who worked at Johnson Cleaners, Ken Lewis at Lennards Shoes, Ken Harris at North's Grocers, Donald Finlayson at Hinton and Lakes Chemist. Charlie Green the Florist had a Van, his driver was Harry Wood, Trumps had several vans and Fields van driver was George Bastin. At Fords was Jim Collins who lived in Sidbury. Fords in those days used to sell Paraffin, which was delivered to quite a large number of customers who lived out in the country areas.

A Life in Sidmouth

I remember one thing that happened one Saturday just as I was leaving work. Mrs Davison, who lived at 'The Sheilings' at the top of Boughmore Road, wanted a pair of shoe laces so off I went to deliver them. On the way I met Ken Harris from Mr North's the Grocers. He was on his way to Captain Moore who lived at 'Edgemond' which was also at the top of Boughmore Road known locally as 'Steep Hill.'

I asked him where he was going and he replied in a despondent voice, 'Captain Moore's. They just rang up for six 'OXO' cubes and it's 6`oclock! What a time to deliver them! I was going to the Cinema early tonight!'

I said, 'I'll take them Ken. I am on my way to 'The Sheilings' which was nearby.'

We boys often helped each other in this way.

Out To Work

Chapter Nine: F T Dunn

F T Dunn

A Life in Sidmouth

I left school at the end of July 1941 to begin a 5 year apprenticeship with the firm of F T Dunn in Sidmouth. The business was situated in Temple Street and consisted of an Ironmongers shop fronting Temple Street, with stores and plumbers workshops at the rear, with access to the workshop off Lawn Vista. The living premises for the family, which consisted of Mr Dunn, his wife and daughter Peggy, were at the rear and above the shop. Also living with them was Mr Dunn's sister Dolly who was a spinster. Dolly and Peggy ran the shop with occasional help from Mr Dunn. He was usually out looking at work and providing estimates for the plumbing side of the business. This side of the business employed two craftsmen and one apprentice, I being the 2nd apprentice, when, I joined the staff.

One must remember we were just going into the third year of the war, and most of the men in the building trade had been called up and were either in the Armed Forces or working in jobs of national importance. Indeed most firms only had a few staff. Most of the men in the town were employed in the building industry prior to the 1939-45 conflict, for the likes of F Pinney & Sons, W J Skinner, E Barnards, E Sanders and Frank Joyce at Sidford. There were also several firm's that carried out plumbing and electrical work, namely; Dunn's, Huck's, Tuckers and Lakes & Son in Old Fore Street, or 'Back Street' to us locals. Lakes used to do all the Sidmouth Manor work, which, back in the 1930s was their major source of work.

One also must remember that before 1932 the Sidmouth Manor owned the town's Water supply. The water supply in those days came from springs situated either above the Golf Course, or from land owned by Sidmouth Manor at the head of the Sid Valley, below Chineway above the village of Sidbury. I have digressed again, so I will return to this again later.

I well remember my first day starting at Dunn's. I left home at 7:35am dressed in new bib and brace overalls and an old sports coat on my drop handlebar bicycle.

It was the custom then for the men to stand on the corner of Lawn Vista at about 7:45am till time to go into the workshop. This seemed to be general practice as Pinney's men were also waiting to go into work by 8am about a 100yds up the road from us. All the time one stood on the corner, the men would acknowledge colleagues going to their place of work somewhere in the area. We would engage in conversation about various subjects, football, rugby and politics, what ever was the interest of the day.

At about 7:55am we would make our way into the workshop and wait for Mr Dunn, the boss, to come out and give us the details of the jobs for the day. This being my first day I was introduced to the two men and the other apprentice who were already employed there.

I was put to work with Maurice Hart. Like me, he had been an apprentice at Dunn's when he left school. The other man working there was a Mr F Holmes, and another apprentice named Elsver Parson.

My first impression was that the workshop was old and dilapidated. The entrance was through two large double doors and there was a window at both ends of the building. There were two long benches, one at right angles to the other and the longest of them was fitted with four large vices. Underneath were drawers for the men to keep tools and each drawer had a lock. At the far end was a double forge, apparently years earlier there had been a blacksmith employed. At one time the firm had always undertaken the work at Vallance's Brewery which was just up the road.

Outside the building set into the surface of the yard were large metal plates as circles which must have been used for making the metal tyres for the horse drawn delivery wagons before the arrival of the motor vehicle. Also in the workshop was a hand operated grinding stone and a bench which held a pipe vice, which we used for holding pipes when cutting threads on the end of a pipe with various different sets of dies. When one looked up at the inside of the roof, hanging down was a type of sling. This held lengths of copper tube of various sizes, there was a rack on the side of the building which contained many lengths of galvanised pipe which I later found out was used on farms etc.

A Life in Sidmouth

Just inside of the building was a landing about nine foot up from the floor, which seemed to be just a dirt floor that had become consolidated over many years, and on this floor was stored sheets of metal of various types, 6 ft x4 ft in size, and of different gauges, or thickness, from 16 to 24 gauge. There was black iron, galvanised iron also rolls of perforated zinc, all used for making articles used in the course of the business. To me it seemed like an 'Aladdin's Cave' at the time.

At about 8:05am Mr Dunn would come out and give us our jobs for the day. On my first day we had to go to Sand House in Sidbury and fix Mrs Sheldon's leaking tap. Our second job was close by at Sand Farm in Roncombe Lane, Sidbury, and we went there to repair a leaking cattle bowl in the cow-shippon. We collected any parts and fittings that were required for the job. Even now I can hear Mr Hart's voice telling me to get this and that and we loaded up all the equipment that we would require in a sack, which Maurice would take. Then he told me to pick up his tool bag and showed me how to fit it on the cross bar of my bicycle with the hammer stem put through the bag's handles so it held the tools while you cycled along.

When we had everything we required we cycled to the job. It all was all so new and strange to me but at the same time exciting. A new phase of my life was starting. The fact that I was going to Roncombe Valley, Sidbury, was in itself an experience, and to someone else's premises was new to me.

When I look back this was the beginning of a change that has influenced the rest of my life. Mr Hart was to have a big effect on my whole life and character.

In the beginning it was Mr Hart this, Mr Hart that, but after a while he said, 'That's enough. Call me by my first name which is Maurice.'

I remember him telling me, 'mind your Ps and Qs when in the customer's houses; no shouting, whistling or lounging about!'

I had never been to this place called Roncombe which was just north of Sidbury Village. It took us about an hour to reach our destination and size up the job. I remember having to wait because the cows were still being milked. After dismantling the drinking bowl we found that our fittings were the wrong size, so I was sent all the way back to the workshop to fetch the right ones. This took another hour or more after which the job was completed.

While back at the workshop, Mr Dunn said, 'When you finish this job tell Maurice to go to Sidbury Manor and I'll meet you there after dinner about starting a new job at the Manor.'

I collected the fittings we required and made my way back to the farm. We completed the job by lunch time, then we went to Sidbury Manor. The house was at this time the residence of Sir Edward Cave and his wife. I well remember cycling down from Roncombe to Sidbury and Maurice explaining and informing me about the Manor, that we always done all the plumbing work on the estate, which consisted of several farms and houses in the village.

In those days practically all the village belonged to the estate. They had their own water supply and they employed several staff. Harry Mitchell was the foreman, Dick Clay was a carpenter, William Maeer was a labourer, Mr Earland was also a carpenter, Ern Taylor was a general worker, Harry Slade was a mason and Jimmy Harris was the Forrester. The yard and workshops were just over the bridge where you turn to go up Lincombe Lane. They used to have their own Saw Mill, with steam engine and saw bench which cut the timber from the estate.

The manor house itself was situated about ¾ of a mile from the village and was approached via a long drive. There are two entrances, and, at each entrance there is a Lodge, the front lodge and back lodge, but the two drives merge into one about ¼ of a mile from each entrance to give you a fine view of the house which is in a slightly elevated position. To the right of the main house are what were once stables and coach houses. When I saw this for the first time I was in awe! I had never seen a house of such size and grandeur before and to think I was going to work there. It was the beginning of a long association with Sidbury Manor, and many hours of employment there.

Sir Edward Cave and his wife had a small staff which consisted of Mr and Mrs Quick. Mr Quick was a sort of butler and general help and his wife was the cook. There was also a lady who came up from the village to clean, a gardener called Sid King who looked after the kitchen garden, and a game keeper who lived in a cottage at the rear of the estate.

As I say, it was a small staff, but one must remember it was wartime, and most of the younger folk had been called up. It must have been very difficult at this time to maintain the standard of upkeep to which the estate was used to. In 1942 the manor was let to Alexandria College, a girl's school from West-Cliff-on-Sea, and for sometime Sir Edward Cave and his mother went to live at The Court Hall in the village.

After a period of time I got the impression that plumbing work seemed to be very territorial. After a time I found this to be true and it became more noticeable as time went on. It seemed that most of our customers were at the higher end of the town in the Sidford, Sidbury area, whereas Lakes mostly carried out work in the western part of the town, possibly because the firm had always been associated with Sidmouth Manor, and had always done their work.

The Sidmouth Manor was responsible for developing the old Sidmouth Water Company. When the springs on the golf links were brought into use and a reservoir at Stintway was built, Messrs Lakes supplied the labour. At a later date 5 inch and 7 inch mains were laid from Virkins Well springs at Horseshoe Plantation, and Ousely Goyle. These are all situated in the upper reaches of the Sid Valley above Sidbury, and were laid by men employed by Lakes.

My time at Dunn's was a happy time and we carried out a variety of work, although one of the disadvantage's was that, this being wartime, there were no new buildings being built due to restrictions. But it also had its benefits. We used to have to repair and make things, which included coal-huds and cowls for fitting on to chimneys which were fitted to control down drafts. We also made quite a lot of flue dampers for use in some of the cottages in Sidbury, which had the old 'ranges' which the tenants cooked on. The Village did not have a Gas Supply before the war and the Water Supply was owned by the Manor Estate. The supply came from three sources Hatway, Lincombe and Darks Moor, which is above Greenhead. We also carried out quite a lot of work on farms which belonged to the estate.

Chapter Ten: War Time

War Time

A Life in Sidmouth

When the Government took over the South Hams area of Devon for training American and British troops in preparations for the D-Day landings, the farmers were moved out and relocated to farms in other areas. One such family of farmers was relocated to Paccombe which was in the Hamlet of Harcombe near Sidford. Our firm did the work and put the cottage and farm buildings into a habitable state.

The cottage and the cow shippons had not been in use for some time, so it was our job to bring them up to the required standard. The work took about six weeks to complete. Each day we would leave the workshop in Temple Street at 8am and cycle to the farm which took us about 40 minutes. We used to take our lunch and a drink, in a thermos-flask, with us. It was quite difficult to make up a lunch because of the food rationing, but something was always conjured up from somewhere. To obtain a 'thermos' you had to apply for a permit from The Food Office, if you were in an occupation that required you to carry your midday lunch.

The family who eventually moved in, I think it was late springtime and they had previously been farming in the South Hams, was called Yabsley. There was Mr and Mrs Yabsley, and two daughters who were married and their husbands were away in the Armed Forces.

The Yabsleys' were lovely people, full of fun. We were still working there when they arrived. They brought all their livestock with them; cows, hens and two pigs, and various agriculture implements. They stayed and farmed till the end of hostilities. After they moved in they always gave us a cup of tea at 10am, at dinner time and again in the afternoon.

When I look back it was a happy period in my life. It was never any trouble cycling out to Paccombe. We only had bicycles in those days but there were things to talk about and observe that was going on in the countryside. A war was raging across Europe and the Far East, but here in East Devon life seemed to go on.

The evacuees had already been here for about two years by now, but as the war progressed, troops were billeted in the town, and most of the large Hotel's were closed and became billets for the various members of the armed forces.

The first regiment was The King's Own, followed by The Royal Engineers. These were then replaced by The Royal Air Force Medical. We also had The Air Force Regiment here. Quite a number of these regiments were billeted with local families in the town. Their officer's mess was at the then Knowle Hotel, now East Devon District Council Offices.

Although we had large numbers of troops in the area we experienced very little social problems. Many of the local families welcomed them into their homes and befriended them. Several local girls got married to the soldiers and when the war was over settled in the town and raised their families.

I can recall that some of the Royal Engineers were billeted in a house called The Myrtles in Millford road and their officers in Devon Cottage, which was next door. There was always a sentry posted at the entrance to the drive by the bridge which leads into the properties and my mother used to make a hot drink for who was on duty, and also a rice pudding which I would take over to them. They would always return the dishes the next day when they were off duty.

Occasionally the troops hired the Parish Hall for a dance on a Saturday night. Quite a few of the men seemed to be from around the South Wales Area. One of the lads went around with one of my sisters. He was from Barry and his mates were also from around that part of Wales. A lad named Charlie Sanger from Cardiff married a local girl, and I remember meeting him eight years later on Cardiff Station, where he was employed as a porter. It's a small world!

It was about this time that my mother was taken ill, and our doctor had to be called to visit her. He confined her to bed for a week and called again a few days later to see how she was. During his visit, my mother mentioned that she had a small lump about the size of a small hazel-nut under her right breast. On examination he told her that she would have to go into the local hospital for further investigations. When these had been carried out, it was found to be breast cancer.

Back then it was not so easily treated. Sidmouth Cottage Hospital used to call on surgeons from the old Royal Devon & Exeter Hospital. Two of the Surgeons at that time were Mr Lock and a Mr Wayland-Smith. Tuesdays and Thursday were operation days at Sidmouth. My mother was operated on and seemed to be making progress, but alas, it did not last, and she eventually passed away on Sunday the 9th of August 1942, aged 54yrs.

During this time we used to have American Airmen coming into the town in the evenings and mostly weekends. They were stationed at Smeatharpe just north of Honiton. They had a large air-base there with US bombers and transporters stationed there. They used to come into the town on their time off looking for girl friends. The Americans were popular with local girls because they had much more money to spend than our boys!

On a few occasions they hired the Parish Hall for dances on a Saturday. I shall never forget those weekends! The waste and the things that went on were disgusting and it was an eye opener to me as a young lad.

As caretakers we had to get the hall ready for them. They would arrive about 11am in an army truck and two jeeps. There would be about 25 men and a couple of officers. During the morning, Vallance's, the local brewery, would deliver about five to six barrels of locally brewed beer. The barrels would be set up on the edge of the stage so that the taps were hanging over the edge.

One Saturday the tap from one of the barrels was leaking and an officer asked if we could lend him a jug to save the beer. We gave him a large jug which held about half a gallon. One of the men was detailed to stand there, save the beer in the jug, and pour it back into the barrel. I thought what a waste of time and good beer. It must have been flat when they came to drink it in the evening? I always thought the Americans were very wasteful, and had no sense of values even though we were in the middle of a war.

There were other instances that made me think how irresponsible they were! To my father and I, it seemed they were never short of any thing; cigarettes were given out like peanuts. On another occasion they had about six cooked hams on the bone and they set up some pint glasses at one end of the hall floor and they played 'skittles' by throwing or skidding the hams along the floor to knock down the glasses at the opposite end. You can imagine the mess on the floor from the fat and breadcrumbs on the joints of Hams. This happened on several occasions, and then my father complained about it.

I also remember that in the road outside in the street there was always a Jeep parked with a couple of Americans in the front seats. They always seemed to arrive about 6:30pm and would park there for the rest of the evening. For several weeks this puzzled me? I began to wonder why they were always there each week.

Every so often an American would go to the Jeep and say something to the occupants in the parked vehicle and request something. I noticed this happing quite often. Being at this tine in my early teens and being on the shy side, I wondered what was going on. After a while my inquisitiveness got the better of me! So I asked one of the men sat in the Jeep, who produced a canvass bag for me to look in, which I did, and I was shocked! It was full of condoms. I leave the rest to the reader's imagination. I was at a loss to say anything. Back then sex, and anything appertaining to it, was taboo, especially to a young fifteen year old!

They had the use of the hall for several weeks but after a time I suppose they moved on to another station. On the last Saturday they used the Hall, as they drove up through the town on their way back to their base at Dunkeswell, they threw out full and empty beer and cider bottle's, that being made of glass, left a dangerous mess behind them.

The Americans were always welcomed by the locals but at times they were a bit on the wild side and resented a little by some of the local lads. But there I suppose, if you have been up rooted and whisked to God knows where, we would perhaps be the same? But on the whole they were not a problem and after all they were here to help us in what were very difficult times.

One or two local girls married Americans and became what was known as GI-Brides. One of them lived around the corner to me in Holmdale, next door to my aunt Mary. My aunt Mary was really my Godmother but we all called her aunt Mary, out of respect, as you did in those days.

The girl was Miss Hatchley. She had been previously married but reverted to her maiden name after her first husband left her. She met her GI boyfriend at a dance, and after he went back to the USA, they wrote to each other for about a year, and then she and her two daughters from the first marriage left Sidmouth and went to the USA when the war ended. She got married to her GI boyfriend in the USA and became Mrs Schultz. She then had another daughter called Mary Lou (Schultz).

In 1959 Mrs Schultz (née Hatchley) wrote to my aunt Mary to enquire if she could find a pen friend for her daughter Mary Lou? Aunt Mary suggested my daughter Sue, who was 10years old at the time. They started writing to each other and have continued to do so for 54 years.

They have met three times now; Mary Lou came over in 1972 and again in 2012. Sue and her husband met Mary Lou in 2009 whilst on holiday in the USA. They were all greeted at the hotel by Fox TV news, CNN TV news and by the South Bend Tribune newspaper on the 6th of June 2009 and interviewed in the reception area.

The various forces remained here for some time until the preparations began for the invasion of the main land of Europe which was planned to take place on the French Coast. The Royal Engineers went to the war front in North Africa under General Alexandria and General Montgomery. They drove the Germans, under Rommel, out of North Africa and this was the turning point of the war.

War Time

When one regiment moved on another regiment would arrive. During the last couple of years before the end of the war the R.A.F. Regiment arrived and the Knowle Hotel, now the East Devon District Council Offices became the Officers mess. Quite a few of the men were billeted out into private accommodation. The R.A.F. Medical Corp came and took over The Salcombe House Hotel. The Westcliffe Hotel and a few other properties were used as sick bays.

With all the troops we had here I must say the town experienced very little trouble. In fact, when the various Regiments moved on, the towns folk were sorry to see them go as many friendships had been made, and, as I have previously mentioned, some had married into local families and settled here after the hostilities ended and had families of their own and still live in the town to this present day. They became employed, and some set up businesses that have contributed to the life and prosperity of the town.

The day that hostilities ceased in Europe the church Bells were rung and the town was in a state of elation. In the evening there were crowds all dancing on the tennis courts at Blackmore and people seemed to be everywhere having a good time singing and dancing till late into the night.

We must remember though, that this was only the end of the war in Europe. The war in the Far East with Japan was still going on. There were many of our local boys out in that war zone, like brothers Arthur and Ernest Leask and also Dick Santer. Some of the lads that came back were in a terrible state.

They not only had to fight the enemy, but also the climate and jungle environment which they were unused to. They were often referred to as the forgotten Army. One follow I knew very well told me it was sheer hell out in the Far East. The Japanese were cruel, ruthless and showed no mercy.

Chapter Eleven: After the War

After the War

A Life in Sidmouth

After a time the town began to return to normal. The first thing that was put into operation was the restoration of the town's hotels that had been taken over. They were returned to their owners, so they could start getting back to the main business of Sidmouth which was the tourist industry, on which the town relied and still does.

F T Dunn, the firm I worked for, was engaged in restoring the Hotel Riviera on the sea front. There were about twenty of us there, electricians and heating engineers from Garton & Kings of Exeter, carpenters and painters from F Pinney & Sons, and carpet fitters from Fields.

The place was like a beehive. Workers names that spring to mind are; Jack Hobbs, Mervyn Fisher, Ken Burnell, George Potter, Dick Pitt, Arthur Jasper and Charlie Gater - all now long gone.

The Ratcliff's owned the Hotel Riviera at that time. They were two sisters and a brother who owned and ran a hotel in Torquay. The two sisters ran the Hotel Riviera in Sidmouth and owned and lived in Rock Cottage, just below Connaught Gardens in Peak Hill Road. The receptionist at the time was Enid Lewis.

In my eyes the Hotel Riviera was always special. Who ever has owned the hotel, it has always been kept in tip-top condition both internally and externally and it adds immensely to the look of our sea-front. I think the hotel was refurbished and reopened in about eight weeks, all ready for the summer season of 1946.

Several months passed before all the hotels were back to the high standard for which the town had been known before the war. Over a period of time things returned to normal.

I have always been proud that I was born here and lived here all my life. It is amazing to my wife and I that where ever you go, either in this country, or to some far off remote place in the world, and you say, 'I'm from Sidmouth,' how often you hear someone say, 'You're lucky to live in such a lovely place!'

After the War

On one occasion I was in London visiting the National Honey Show where I was exhibiting some of my honey and I was introduced to two of the top judges. On being asked were I was from, on the mention of Sidmouth, they said, 'You come from one of the loveliest and cleanest seaside towns in England!'

I was so proud of such a compliment about the town which I have lived in now for over 83yrs, and have never had any desire to leave.

The end of the war was to have far reaching effects on my life.

My mother had died on the 9th of August 1942, and when it was realised that my mother was not going to recover from the breast cancer, my eldest sister Margaret came back home. She had been in domestic service at the home of the Reverend and Mrs Nightingale at Salcombe Close in Sid Lane, Sidmouth where she had been employed since she left school in 1927.

My other two sisters, who were twins, were in the forces. Irene had joined the ATS, and Rose who had earlier gone to South Wales to work in a munitions factory, had left and joined the women's naval service known as the Wrens and was stationed in Greenock Scotland.

My sister Margaret was so different from my mother. I thought being in domestic service for 15yrs she would have been trained in running a house but she became a disappointment in more ways than one.

My mother was good at every thing and was a very resourceful person in all manner of ways. She took in washing to supplement the family income; she used to make clothes for herself and my sisters when they were going to school and she always knitted socks for my father and I. The only thing she ever took to Mr Marks, the tailor, aside from the ladies raincoat previously mentioned, was my trousers. She used to have them, what she called, re-seated, when a large round patch of similar material was fitted. I hated this but most boys had it done. I must say if you had the cane at school you didn't feel it so much!

My mother always made us good meals and I can still remember what we had; Mondays was usually bubble and squeak; Tuesdays we had a salad in summer or pea soup in winter and Wednesdays it was 'navvies-waistcoat' which was the nick name for a breast of mutton.

A few years ago I was in our local butchers. There were several ladies waiting to be served and the butcher asked me what I wanted.

I said, 'Two navvy's-waistcoats please.'

He disappeared out the back of the shop to get them.

Our local doctor's wife was there and she said, 'What was that you asked for?'

I told her but she had never heard of them being referred to by that name.

My mother made the most delicious veal and ham pies. In the winter on Saturdays we always had her home made steak and kidney pudding, they were super, 'Oh yes!' There was always fish once or twice a week either for dinner or tea, mackerel when in season, and always herrings in the winter. When we had plaice it was always fried on the bone. We also had pollack, whiting, rock-salmon (known locally as 'duncow') and sprats. I don't ever remember having cod except if we went and got fish and chips from Charlie Parrot's down York Street.

There was no doubt my mother had been a good wife to my father and a good and loving mother to my sisters and me. I wondered at the time how her passing would affect my father, but after a time he got over her loss. At the time my father was 60yrs old, but with his work and his allotments, going to the rugby on Saturday things eventually returned to normal.

My eldest sister Margaret ran the house but as I said not very, what's the word, efficiently. After my mother died my father who had a joint bank account with my mother changed it into a joint account with my sister. There was not a lot of money in the account, but, not being careful and thrifty like my mother; my father found she had gradually spent nearly all of his savings. My father, who was a very forgiving man, had a few words over it but the matter was soon forgotten about.

During this time things went on has normal. My father and I just accepted that my sister was no replacement for my mother but we coped.

My sister Margaret was now 29 and she had had one boy friend about 3yrs years previous but nothing came of it. He was a farm worker from Branscombe and she went with him for a couple of years. I think she was more interested in going to my Aunt's, gossiping and going to the Cinema than anything else.

She met someone else but this did not last long. Eventually she met someone from Wellington in Somerset whom she had known through a friend a few years previously. After a time they got married and she left home to live there. He was in the Army but after the war he went back to his old job as milkman with the local Co-Operative Society. They ended up having a large family of six or seven children including two sets of twins.

They were both happy but I never thought he showed much love to me, there was something missing. They lost one of their twin girls when very young and we seemed to drift apart, but her children were very close to their mother and later in life the children got on in the world of work. Her husband had some health problems and had to have both his legs amputated at his knees. This as one can imagine was a great shock and handicap, but they lived to a good age.

Air Raid Precautions, or ARP, was a system set up prior to the start of the war in all cities, towns and villages. A Central Command was set up which co-ordinated the various services such as Fire, Rescue, Ambulance and First-Aid, Red Cross and the Police. The members of these different sections were already members of these organisations and members of the public also joined and were given the necessary training.

What used to happen was, when the siren sounded to warn that there were enemy planes in the vicinity, you went to the post you were attached to. The main Control Centre in Sidmouth was at Church House, now Kennedy House. The persons in charge in Sidmouth were a retired Army Captain named Thullis, and Mr Ron Boyce, a well known local jeweller. They were responsible for co-ordinating the above services.

About this time I met a young lady who joined the ARP and became a messenger at the ARP post were I was also a messenger. This was in 1942.

Our post was at the old National Provincial Bank in the High Street. At that time it was operating as a working bank and the Manager was Mr J Mummery. The staff at our ARP post consisted of a head warden and six general wardens, who's duties were to go out on patrol, in pairs, in the area we were responsible for.

During the six years we were in operation, except for two incidents, nothing happened!

On one occasion some German planes fired tracer bullets over the town and on another they dropped some bombs in the Bickwell Valley area. One of these bombs landed in the field in front of the Convent. If it had hit the Convent it would have been a major tragedy as the convent had about 30 to 40 nuns living there at the time plus about 30 schoolchildren who were boarders. The road in Bickwell Valley was hit by a bomb which damaged the water main serving the area, and the property called 'Westwards' occupied by Colonel Hudson had part of the veranda destroyed as well as the rear of the house. The water main serving the area was blown up.

To return to my, shall I say, girl friend, sweetheart, or just friend? We were both in our early teens, and at first we became just good friends. When I look back I think she felt sorry for me because I had just lost my mother. Our friendship developed and we became more than just friends, one could say we fell in love with each other.

We used to go cycling together and always went to the pictures once a week. During the summer months we would go on picnics on our cycles. I remember cycling to Exeter Airport on a couple of occasions. We went swimming after the end of the war when the beaches were cleared of the anti invasion devices that had been installed at the beginning of the war.

Sometimes on a Friday evening after she had left work, she would come to the house and prepare a pie for my father and I to have for lunch on Saturday. On Sundays we always went for walks and would come back to our house to have tea with my dad. She was a very homely sort of girl. She had three sisters all older than her, and three brothers, two who were older than herself and one younger.

We went on holiday for a week to my sister Irene, in Dartford Kent. My sister had moved here after her husband had been demobbed from the RAF Regiment. He was a native of Stone just south of Dartford.

Though we got on well we did have our little tiffs. One of her sisters married a soldier and they went back to his home town of South Shields after the end of the war when he was demobbed. Her sister was a lovely person full of the joys of spring! After a couple of years she was expecting a baby, so it was suggested my girlfriend go up and look after her during her confinement. She went a couple weeks before the baby was due, and stayed for a few weeks afterwards.

While she was there she met her sister's husband's younger brother and fell in love with him. After she returned to Sidmouth he moved down here to live and they married. He was a carpenter by trade and he eventually set up his own business. He was also a very keen boxer and helped restart the Sidmouth Boxing Club which had closed down at the outbreak of the war. We had been very close, so this came as a wrench. My father was upset at the time, but I got over it as did he.

About this time some new people, who had come to live in the town, suggested we should have a youth club in Sidmouth. Several meetings were, called and a Youth Club was formed. The two people most involved in setting the club up were Mr Kayzer Leach and the Reverend Hines, who I think was a Unitarian Minister.

The club was eventually formed and used to meet on a Thursday evening at the Drill Hall. I became a member along with several other lads I knew. In the early days we had a membership of about sixty. We used to have some coach trips and they also decided to put on a show to raise funds. I well remember the audition; we had a rehearsal for singing.

A Mr Livesley who took us for the singing, said, 'Who is the person with the deep base voice?'

It was me. He said, 'You stand at the back and just go ba ba.'

It put me off, so I dropped out and that was the end of my musical career.

I was asked if I would organise some Sunday walks for the Youth Club, which I agreed to do.

The first walk I organized was to Branscombe. We met at 2pm at Alma Bridge, we walked up the Cliff path to Salcombe Hill on via the cliff path to Salcombe Mouth, Weston, and then on to Branscombe Beach. After some refreshments, in the beach café, and some games on the beach, it was time to make tracks for our return walk back to Sidmouth. Our return route was through the lane into the village square, past the pub 'The Masons Arms,' still a popular hostelry at the time of writing, and up through the long winding village past the Norman Church on or right. The village of Branscombe is one of the longest villages in England.

After the War

The village also had a local Bakery which was owned and run by the Collier family. The bread, which tasted like no other bread, was made in the old traditional way and baked in ovens which used the old fashion method of being heated by large faggots, or, what the uninformed would call, bundles of wood. These would be put in and set alight and when burnt out they would be swept out and the bread ready for the ovens would be placed in the oven until cooked. This bread tasted like no other bread in the area.

The village also had its own blacksmith. Both these businesses are carried on today. The Bakery is now maintained and own by The National Trust.

We continued our walk back to Sidmouth via Weston, Dunscombe and Trow Hill to Sidford, where we dispersed. Most seemed to have enjoyed their time and requested I arrange another in a month's time, and again, this I agreed to do.

For my second walk, I planned to meet at Exeter Cross and to walk along Manstone Lane, Burscome Lane to Hollow Head, and onto White Cross down into Tipton- St- John and back along the River Otter. But alas, I think I overdone it on the first walk, and on this occasion only 10 turned up to walk. They had lots of enthusiasm and they completed the walk and enjoyed it. But that was the last walk we did. I can only assume I had over done it and tired them all out!

The youth club lasted for quite a few years. We had coach trips and we also used to go cycle trips to Exmouth and Seaton. Several of the members found their future wifes and husbands through the club.

Some of us went our own ways, I paled up with Gerald Bess and John and Chris Andrews. They were all keen sportsmen and eventually played football for Sidmouth. I went to play for Sidbury United. On Sunday we would go down on The Ham and play with others in a friendly knock about.

Chapter Twelve: July 1948

July 1948

A Life in Sidmouth

In the summer I played tennis in the evenings and on Saturday afternoons, and it was through this that I first met the girl who was to become my future wife. I'd been playing tennis one Saturday afternoon with Gerald Best, Graham Hooke and John Andrews, and I had left them and walked up from the courts at the Coburg Pleasure Ground, past the hospital and along the top of All Saints Road into Radway, and I suppose I was outside the cinema when I saw my friend Eddie Newberry, who I was going 'mushrooming' with at 4am the following morning.

He was talking with a young lady on her bicycle and I said in passing, 'See you in the morning.'

'Okay!' he replied.

He introduced me to her. She looked at me and I smiled at her, and I left them talking.

Next morning I said, 'Who was that you were with?'

He said, 'Just someone I know. She wanted to know who you were but I told her, 'You don't want to know him!''

Anyway I never thought anymore about it. That must have been the first Saturday in July 1948, and three weeks later, on the 24 July, I'd been up to see my friends Maurice Hart and his wife. After visiting them I went down to the fair, which came to the town for four days each year. It was sited in the field opposite the left hand side of what is now Coulsdon Road. I went in and stood on the steps of the bumper-cars to watch.

Off to my right hand side I saw Margaret Vincent, a girl I had known through the youth club, and there with her was the girl I had previously seen talking to my friend outside the Radway Cinema.

Apparently, I didn't know, but Magaret's mother had three daughters and was Welsh, and they lived at Sidford in a house called Terranova and Vera used to go and visit them once a week.

Anyway, there she was with Margaret. Whether it was intentional or no I don't know, but Margaret Vincent said, 'Well, I'll leave, I'm off,' she said, 'I'm going home Vera, I'll leave you with Gerald, I think you've met before.'

So there we were stood together on the edge of the bumping cars.

Eventually I said, 'Would you like to have a go on the bumping cars with me?'

I didn't have a lot of money on me and I was worried I didn't have enough in my pocket.

Vera said, 'Yes, alright!'

So in we got, the bumper cars started and we went bumping into everybody as we went and as everybody always did.

We had a couple of rides and then we wandered around the other attractions and I said, 'Where are you going now?'

She said, 'I'm going home.'

I asked, 'Where do you live?'

Vera replied, 'Oh, I live in Manstone Avenue, 212.'

212 was down the bottom end. I found out she was lodging there away from her home in Wales.

I asked, 'Can I walk up the road with you?'

She said yes and we both started walking up Yarde Hill pushing our bicycles along.

I asked, 'Any chance of seeing you on Saturday and go in the picture house, go to the pictures?'

But she said, 'Sorry, my cousin is coming from Wales to meet me in Exeter on Saturday.'

I replied, 'Perhaps some other time?'

She said she couldn't put her cousin off as it was now Thursday and her cousin had booked her seat on the train in Cardiff. I was a bit disappointed, but that was that. I asked if she was working in Sidmouth and she said she worked in Woolworths in the town. With that we parted. I thought she looked disappointed, I was. I thought she was a nice type of girl and not the flighty sort.

I went to work next morning wondering if I should see her going to work on her bicycle, or going home in the evening but it was not to be. Next day being Saturday we finished at 12pm and the afternoon was given up to tennis with the lads. All the time she was running through my mind and how can I see her again. Then I wondered if she already had a boy friend?

Anyway, I found out two or three months later that the cousin that was coming from Cardiff was really an ex-boyfriend she was going with who lived in a village called Penygraig whom she had met at a dance back in the Rhondda Valley. He was a pharmacist who worked for Boots the Chemists, so I didn't think I had much of a chance. She was honest with me and told me this herself quite a few months afterwards.

On Sundays some of the lads and I always went to watch the cricket. My thoughts kept coming back to her and our chance meeting at the fair that previous Thursday.

Anyway, Sunday and Monday came and went. Going back to work gave me something to think about, but on the Wednesday lunch time I went into Woolworth's to see if she was there.

She was behind the counter serving a lady. I waited until she had finished serving the customer and spoke to her and asked if we could meet up sometime .We agreed to meet outside the Radway Cinema at 7pm on the following Saturday.

I'm afraid I didn't go up to Manstone to meet her, but I was there waiting for her when she came down on the bus. I remember she was wearing a light green spotted dress, which I believe was printed with a white pattern of small daisy-like flowers.

We greeted each other and I said, 'It's nice to see you, I've been looking forward to this,' and I asked her if she would prefer to go for a walk or to the pictures?

She said she would like to go to the cinema so in we went. I can't quite remember the show, I've got a suspicion it was James Cagney and 'Yankee Doddle Dandee', and in fact I'm almost certain it was.

Anyway, we went to the pictures and I always remember each time we went to the pictures after that I always bought her a ¼lb box of Milk-Tray from 'Screw-Fart' Fields, the tobacconist, sweet and grocery shop, next to the Radway Inn on the corner of Salcombe Road. Everyone called him 'Screw-Fart' Fields. I don't know why, it was his nickname I think. Anyway I always remember buying a ¼lb box of Milk-Tray which was at the time 1/6d.

So we sat there watching the film, we were both too shy to say much to each other. The film finished about 10pm and every one trooped out.

Then I said, 'I will walk home with you.'

She replied, 'That would be nice!'

I asked her if she had to be in her lodgings by a certain time and she replied, 'The people I stay with are very good and don't restrict what time I get in, within reason, and I have my own key.'

My immediate thoughts were that she must be a nice type of person for them to let her hold her own key. I suggested to her that we walk home by going up All Saints Road, Station Road and down Alexandria Road, which would bring us out to Manstone where she lived. So off we went walking side by side chatting away, and eventually she caught hold of my arm. The footpath in Station Road is raised above the road and in those days there were a few seats along it.

After a while we sat down on one for a rest. We sat there and had a kiss and a cuddle. I wanted to find out more about her so I asked her where was she from? She said her name was Vera Sheppard, she was Welsh, and came from the Rhondda Valley from a place called Treherbert, and that she was currently working in Woolworths. She said she had previously worked in the Eagle Restaurant in Fortfield Terrace and she told me the history of how she came to Sidmouth.

She had come to Sidmouth with her sister's friend Rose, whom her sister had met in the WAFs during the war. Apparently her sister, Gwen, and her friend Rose intended to set up a little tea and coffee shop somewhere on the south coast. Gwen had worked in her brother's grocery shop in the village of Tynewydd, The India & China Tea Company, in the Welsh valleys before the war, and he wanted his sister back to help build up the business after the war.

Vera, who started to train as a nurse at the local Hospital in Treherbert, had had a nervous break-down and had been home for some considerable time due to this illness.

So it was decided that Gwen would stay with her brother and Vera would go with Rose, who had seen an advert in the magazine, 'The Lady,' asking for two staff for a restaurant that was opening in Sidmouth Devon. They both applied for the positions and were successful. They started at the restaurant in Easter 1946.

This must have been quite an experience for Vera who had never been away from her home in Treherbert in the South Wales Valley. She told me her mother was quite upset about her leaving Wales and going to England, another Country!

The Eagle Restaurant was situated in Fortfield Terrace, which was Sidmouth's well known Regency Terrace. The building, which is No 6, has an emblem of the Russian Eagle on the front facia, and at one time, the then Empress of Russia stayed here.

Rose, who was the older of the two girls, arrived a fortnight before Vera to help prepare and sort things out. Vera told me she got off the bus from Exeter in All Saints Road, and went into a restaurant in the High Street, called 'The Beehive,' which is now Fulfords Estate Agents.

She wasn't very impressed, and thought, 'If this is Sidmouth I won't be staying!'

She is still here after 65yrs! She eventually arrived at The Eagle Restaurant in Fortfield Terrace. The restaurant, which was a new venture, was opened by Miss Dugdale and another lady and later owned by Mr and Mrs W Small. Vera was taken and shown her accommodation as both her and Rose were to live in on the premises. Their bedrooms were on the top floor of the house with lovely views out to sea.

The builders, J & W Skinners, were still working there doing alterations. Names of some of the workmen there were; Bill Inch, Charlie Broom, Eddie Newberry and Peter Selley. Vera used to smuggle them a cup of tea whenever she could.

She told me her weekly wage was £1 a week plus all her tips, which was always very good. The restaurant was very select and did not have coach trippers. One could have morning coffee or tea, and they also did lunches and Sunday lunches. About 50yards along the road was the Sidmouth Cricket Tennis and Croquet Club and this no doubt brought them a good class of clientele, and plenty of trade in the summer period.

Vera also told me about her father, Frederick Sheppard.

He worked in the mines as a 'banksman' who would let the men down in the cages and checked they didn't have any cigarettes or matches. Also, when the coal came up in the coal drams, as they called them, he was responsible for weighing them and checking them so they knew what each gang produced so it could be calculated what they would be paid. Each gang had their name on the side of the dram.

She also told me that her father originally came from Langport in Somerset and was a farmer. Her mother's name was Celia Sheppard (née Jenkins) and they were also a farming family. I found out afterwards from her father, that he left to work in the Welsh coalfields during the agricultural depression back in the early 1900s.

Anyway Vera and I got on well. She asked me about myself and she said, 'I always looked on you as the boy with the rhubarb!'

My friend that I learned my trade with, Maurice Hart, and his wife, were like a second father and mother to me. Maurice taught me amateur photography, and we used to go out walking together taking pictures. Both Maurice and his wife had quite an influence on my character.

My father and I had an allotment, and whenever there were some spare vegetables I used to take them up to Maurice on a Sunday morning. This included rhubarb when it was in season. We had a lot of rhubarb on the allotment and I used to cycle up to Mr and Mrs Hart with about ten sticks of rhubarb under my arm.

Vera used to see me pass on my bicycle and this is why she used to refer to me as the boy with the rhubarb under his arm!

We talked for some time and then I said, 'I think it's time I took you home.'

So we walked back to 212 Manstone Avenue where she lodged. I told her about my self and that I lived with my father, that I was a plumber, had always lived in the town and that I had three sisters who all lived away.

By this time it was about 11:30pm. I took her to the front door and she squeezed my arm. I gave her a kiss and asked if we could meet up again.

'Yes,' she said, 'I will meet you tomorrow at the Triangle about 2pm,' and with that she squeezed my hand and slipped in the front door.

The following morning I made a few rock-cakes and some sandwiches, cheese I think, and I duly went and met her off the bus at the Triangle.

'Where would you like to go,' I said.

Vera replied, 'I don't mind.'

So we went up Peak Hill, walked to just below Peak Cottage and went out on to the cliff edge. Back then there was a small triangular piece of grass about five yards square that was very secluded. You went through a gap in the hedge on the edge of the road, just west a bit from the junction of Cotmaton Road where Peak Hill Road veers north-west away from the coastline. This part of the road was known locally as Wind Whistle Corner.

We didn't stay there long as I detected that Vera was a little nervous sitting so close to the cliff edge.

I said, 'You are not happy here.'

So we moved to the top of the field immediately above Connaught Gardens. After a while a couple of pigeons came and settled by us, so she wanted to move down the field. Every time we moved the birds followed us.

I explained that they were quite harmless, and then I said, 'I have brought some tea for us. It's not much, a few cakes and sandwiches, and a thermos of tea.'

'I wondered what you had in your carrier,' she said.

'It's not much. I prepared it myself. My father and I live on our own.'

'Yes,' she said, 'someone told me that. I think it was the lady I lodge with. Her daughter-in-law lives with them and she knows you because you came into the shop where she used to work, to get your bread.'

After moving from the top of the field to bottom, I said, 'It's time we had the tea I've brought.'

'I could do with a cuppa,' she said.

So I poured the tea into the cups I had and opened the little box with the sandwiches which we ate and I hope she enjoyed. While we were having tea I raised the matter of moving every time any pigeons or birds came near us and Vera confessed that she was terrified of birds. Apparently, when she had her nervous breakdown, when she was nursing, all she could see were masses of birds flying at her and she still had a complex about birds, which has always stayed with her.

After our snack we talked about our life and families. She told me she had often seen me going up the road on a Sunday and wondered who I was.

She used to say to the people she lodged with, 'Who is that boy? He goes up past here every Sunday and always has rhubarb under his arm.'

I told her that I always went up to see my friend Mr Hart who was the man I had been put with to train as a plumber. Mr Hart also got me interested in amateur photography, and both he and his wife treated me like a second son. I think because I had lost my mother they took some interest in me. They had a son of their own. His name was Raymond and he was 6 yrs old then. He was born in 1942.

Anyway, one thing led to another and we eventually became deeper involved with each other and we started going out on a regular basis and we hit it off. Most of our courtship was spent, I suppose, going to the cinema once a week and wandering around the hills and the walks of Sidmouth.

I remember one Thursday evening. We walked from Manstone right up over the top, through the fields and over the top through the brambles to the top of Core Hill which is an old ancient fort. The views from there are wonderful. We sat down, had a kiss and a cuddle, as we did in most places, and we got on like a house on fire.

This went on for a couple of weeks and then my father said to me one evening, 'You'd better bring her in!'

I lived with my father at this time because my mother had died when I was about 14 years old and my sisters had all left home. They had all met people in the Forces and got married. My father and I were on our own but we looked after ourselves well. Better not put in about the false teeth had I? (*Gerald starts laughing*).

Anyway, so one night I took her down to meet my dad and I sometimes wonder if Vera didn't fall in love with him! She worshipped my father. She thought he was one of the most wonderful men she had ever met. My father was easy to get on with and never lost his temper. He was the most placid person.

We carried on our courtship. In the summer, until the end of September, we used to go over to the Connaught Gardens, sit in the deck-chairs and listened to the Sidmouth Town Band because my friend Maurice had played with them from when he was about 16 years old, as did his father before him, for all his life. Maurice was into everything actually, including the ambulance service, and during the war the rescue service.

Then my father said to me one day, my father was the same as I was I suppose, broad Devon accent, 'Bring the maid in one Saturday night after pictures and I'll get some fish and chips and keep them warm in the oven.'

My father always referred to her as the maid.

So I said to Vera when we came out of the Grand Cinema one night, 'Dad said to come down and you can have a bit of supper.'

So we walked home and father had the table all laid, knives and forks and that. There were no serviettes, we didn't stand for it, we never got to that standard. And we had fish and chips that he kept warm in the oven. He'd been down to Charlie Parrot's fish and chip shop down York Street, which is a pity, no longer exists.

One Sunday we went for a walk and went into The Marlborough Restaurant, Dukes today, for a coffee, and then we went up to The Connaught Gardens to listen to the Sidmouth Town Band. Back then, in 1948, they gave a concert on Wednesday and Sunday evenings for summer visitors in the town. During their interval I took the opportunity to introduce Vera to Maurice.

Vera and Maurice seem to click straight away. She being Welsh and having been involved in singing and music in general, they got on like a house on fire, to use an expression. We met him again after the programme for a short chat and Vera told me how nice he was.

When we left the gardens we walked back across the sea front and I took her back to her lodgings. We agreed to meet up again on the next day which was Bank Holiday Monday. The arrangements were that we would go and walk through Harpford Woods, I would provide tea for both of us and we would meet at 'Big-Bum Churchill's Corner' in Woolbrook, which is at the junction of Manstone Avenue and Woolbrook Road.

Apparently, a Mr Churchill lived in the first house to the west of the junction, but why it is known as 'Big-Bum Churchill's Corner' I'll leave to your imagination.

The day turned out a complete disaster in more ways than one and it was the only time Vera and I had a real disagreement.

I'd made some scones and sponge cake which I was quite capable of doing, and I was going to take her out to Harpford Woods and have a picnic. When I woke up on the Monday morning in question, it was overcast and looked like rain. The rain started a couple of hours later about 10am and it teemed down and never stopped all day.

Anyway, I kept my promise and at about 2pm I got on my bicycle and rode up to our agreed meeting place and waited for approximately half an hour. I didn't take the food because of the weather. I intended we could have gone back on the bus somewhere down the town for a coffee but she never turned up. I never saw her anyway.

She insisted later that she'd turned up and that's the only disagreement I can say, that we really had in our courtship.

So I made my way home saddened to say the least. I was wet through and felt utterly miserable.

I had no means of contacting her. I thought of going to her lodgings but she and I were both shy and had only recently met and I thought I might embarrass her so I decided against it. The rain continued until about 4pm when it cleared and the sun came out.

My father and I had our tea. I read one of my books, listened to the radio or something, and about half-past five, a quarter-to six, I went out to town with the intention of eventually cycling up to see Vera.

A Life in Sidmouth

I knew where she lived but I'd never been there before. I knew the people she was lodging with in Sidmouth. Anyway, I got up by the Grand Cinema and there was a queue there waiting to go in to see the film and about half-past six and there was Vera with Mildred, a friend who was the daughter in law of Mr and Mrs Thomas where she lodged in Manstone Avene.

I went up to them and said to Vera, 'What happened to you this afternoon?'

Vera gave me the cold shoulder and I sensed she was not to happy with me. The queue then started to move and Vera and Mildred went on into the Cinema. I was not very popular!

Mildred was also Welsh. Mr and Mrs Thomas's son, Mervyn, was a gunner in the Royal Air Force. Mildred was his wife and they had a baby boy with blonde hair. I actually knew Mildred because I used to go into Broughton's to get our bread everyday and Mildred used to serve in the shop to supplement their income. Sadly, Mervyn, was shot down and killed and Mildred was left a widow.

Anyway, Vera went there and lodged with them when the Eagle Restaurant closed down. Vera then left and went back home to Wales but Mr and Mrs Thomas thought a lot of her and her friend Mildred who lived further round the same Welsh Valley. So, Mrs Thomas went to Wales to see them and their families and persuaded them to come back to Sidmouth. It was after she came back to Sidmouth that I first met Vera.

The following evening I went around to the rear of Woolworth's where the staff came out after closing. Vera came out with her bicycle and I over to her.

She smiled and said, 'I didn't expect to see you again!'

I said, 'I have come to apologise for what went wrong yesterday.'

'You didn't turn up!' she said.

I replied, 'I Went up to 'Big-Bum Churchill's Corner' on my bike but there was no sign of you so I went home.'

Vera didn't believe me.

I said, 'Lets not fall out about it, I am sorry.'

Vera then said, 'But it was a terrible day. It rained all day; we could not have gone on a picnic!'

I replied, 'No, I suppose not.'

'Anyway what have you come round here for,' she quickly added.

I said, 'I wanted to see you again and see if you wanted to go out with me again?'

Vera said, 'Well, I am off home now to my lodgings for tea. How about meeting tomorrow evening about 7 pm? I will see you on the corner of Manstone Avenue by the GPO telephone kiosk.'

'Yes, that will be alright,' I said.

'Don't forget to turn up!' she said as she got on her bike and rode off.

She didn't look back. I watched until she turned the corner and was out of sight and I was thrilled inside. She wanted to see me again. I could not wait for tomorrow evening to come and I could see her again.

The following evening came and she was there at our agreed meeting place. We went for a long walk up to Core Hill via Coreway and back through Core Lane, down past Colonel Hine-Haycock's, into Woolbrook Road and back to her lodgings.

By this time it was past 10 o'clock. We had a little kiss, and then I made my way home. I thought that Monday's episode was behind us and our feelings for each other were very strong. We agreed to meet again.

Our next date was the following Saturday evening when we went to the Radway Cinema. We agreed to meet out side the cinema at 7pm. Vera would come down on the bus and I would be on the corner of All Saints Road to meet her before she arrived. On the way to meet her I would go to Fields the tobacconist and sweet shop next to the Radway Inn, now an Indian takeaway, and buy her the usual ¼lb box of Milk Tray chocolates. This became routine whenever we went to the cinema. Vera always insisted that I had a share of them.

When we came out after the film, at about 9:50pm, I proposed that I would walk her back to her lodgings in Manstone Avenue. I asked what time she had to be in by but she used to have her own key in case she was late.

I asked her, 'Which way would you like to walk home?

'I will leave it to you,' she said, 'there is no hurry.'

So we went off along All Saints Road, up Station Road and along the footpath which was higher than the road and avoids the traffic. Halfway along this path we sat and had a chat. I wanted to get to know more about Vera and about her family and how she came to Sidmouth in 1946 from her home in the Rhondda Valley.

Anyway, she told me quite a bit about her family. I think she thought I was a gas-bag doing an interview, vetting her and that, you know. I found her very passionate, I'll say that much. We sat on that seat and I can remember every minute. We must have stayed on that seat for an hour. And then she told me she had two sisters and a brother. As I mentioned her brother was the manager of the old Indian & China Tea Company.

Anyway our romance developed from there and eventually she came home to my father to that fish and chips supper and that and then my life was about to make a dramatic turn.

July 1948

A Life in Sidmouth

Gerald Counter - Water Inspector
Image ©Gerald M Counter

EAST DEVON WATER BOARD

This certifies that Mr. G. Counter   is an
authorised Officer, within the meaning of the Water
Act 1945 - 3rd Schedule - Section 62 - Waste
Detection, to enter upon any premises supplied by
the Board in order to examine for waste or mis-use
of water. The bearer may **not** enter private premises
during the hours of darkness without the permission
of the occupier.

46, New Street,
HONITON.
TEL. Honiton 556/7

A.M.I.C.E., A.M.I.W.E.,
Chief Engineer

East Devon Water Board
Authorisation to enter premises
Image ©Gerald M Counter

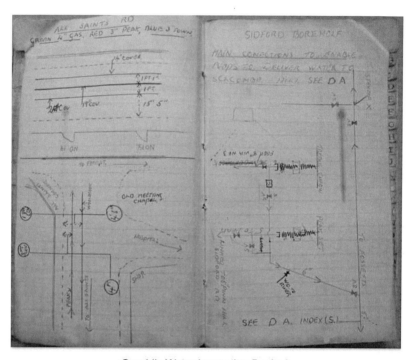

Gerald's Water Inspection Books I
Image ©Gerald M Counter

A Life in Sidmouth

Gerald's Water Inspection Books II
Image ©Gerald M Counter

INCOME TAX YEAR 1947-48

**CERTIFICATE OF PAY
AND TAX DEDUCTED**

G. Counter

(Name of employee and Works No., if any)

Code No. at 5 April, 1948

(Enter "E" if an Emergency
Card is in use at 5 April, 1948)

District
Refce.
(if any)

			Gross pay			Tax		
1. Pay and tax in respect of previous employment(s) in 1947-48 taken into account in arriving at the tax deductions made by me/us			£	s.	d.	£	s.	d.
			181	2	9	4	1	0
2. PAY AND TAX IN MY/OUR EMPLOYMENT								

I/We certify that the particulars given above include the total amount of pay (including overtime, bonus, commission, etc.) paid to you by me/us in the year ended 5 April, 1948, and the total tax deducted by me/us (less any refunds) in that year.

F T Dunn ....Employer

....................Date

TO THE EMPLOYEE. Keep this certificate. It will help you to check the Notice of Assessment which the tax office will send you in due course.

P60

F T Dunn P60 1947-8
Image ©Gerald M Counter

20th November 1956

FROM
SIR CHARLES CAVE,
ESTATE OFFICE,
SIDBURY,
DEVON.
TELEPHONE: 223 & 244

Dear Mr. Counter,

I much appreciated the work that you put in earlier this year when you helped us with our water shortage on the Filcombe supply, and I will be very glad if you are able to come to the Audit Dinner at the Royal Oak tomorrow evening 21st November at 7.30 pm.

Yours truly
C.E.Cave

Invitation to Gerald Counter
by Sir Charles Cave
to the Court Leet Annual Dinner
at the Royal Oak in November 1957
Image ©Gerald M Counter

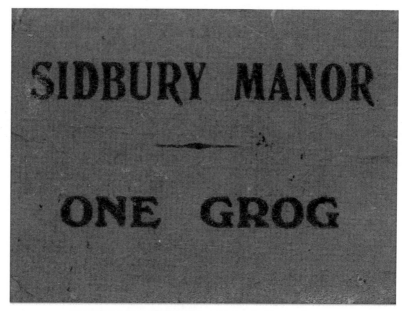

'Grog' ticket given to Gerald Counter by Sir Charles Cave
with the invitation to the Court Leet Annual Dinner
at the Royal Oak in November 1957
Image ©Gerald M Counter

A Life in Sidmouth

Renovation at Witheby c.1946
Rear L-R: Alfie Tapley - Ivor Dunn - boy nk - Jimmy 'Bang-Bang' - Sid Broom.
Front L-R: Bill Inch - Freddie Hoare - Eddie Newberry.
Renovation of Witheby (House) in Cotmaton Road
after evacuees left after WWII so that Mr & Mrs Schrodder could return.
Image ©Gerald M Counter

South West Water Plc.

This Certificate

was presented

to
Gerald Mark Counter

by The Chairman and Directors

as a mark of appreciation

on retirement

following 41 *years of loyal*

service in The Water Industry

Date 26 October 1990

Chairman

Gerald's Certificate for 41years
loyal service In the Water Industry
Image ©Gerald M Counter

'The Squire' (Gerald Counter)
Image ©Gerald M Counter

A Life in Sidmouth

Chapter Thirteen: On Loan

On Loan

A Life in Sidmouth

I went back to work on the Tuesday after August Bank Holiday 1948, and like we always did, we all queued up outside, well not all of us, there was only about three of us, and then went in the workshop to get our orders for the day.

My boss, Mr Dunn, of F T Dunn of Temple Street, the plumbers, said to me, 'Gerald, Bert Scadding, the manager of the Sidmouth Urban District Council (SUDC) Water Department, wants to borrow somebody and I think you're the best one to go because you finished your job last week and the others are still ongoing with theirs. They want you to go up to their office at Woolcombe Lane at the junction with Lawn Vista.'

That's where the SUDC Water Department and Council Yard was then before they built the present flats and toilets in Lawn Vista at the back of the Police Station.

I had my boiler-suit on, I picked up my tools from the bench in the workshop, and then got on my bicycle with my tools and made haste and went up to see Mr Scadding whom I had met before as a young boy when he was a Scout Master.

The way he greeted me was, 'I want you to do some jobs, fix some water meters and one or two other jobs. But the first thing you can do is go home and take your boiler-suit off, put some decent clothes on, have your breakfast and come back here at 9 o'clock.'

I'd already had my breakfast but I went home to change clothes. This turned out to be general procedure with the Sidmouth Water Department. So I went back at 9 o'clock with my grey trousers and check sports coat on.

'Ah! That looks better,' he said. 'I want you to go with Mr Lake.'

Peter Lake was the foreman. 1948 was quite a reasonable summer and Peter Lake and I went round the hotels asking the managers to conserve water and also to look for any over-flows, or anything like that, any wasted water. I immediately got on well with

Peter Lake but I found there was a bit of friction between the Lakes and Mr Scadding.

The Lake family had been involved in the water industry in Sidmouth for years. One of them had a plumbing business in Old Fore Street and used to do the plumbing work for the Water Company. He had two brothers, one was Ernest Lake, Peter's father, and he had been the old water manager until he retired in 1948, and Scadding, who was in the office of the Sidmouth Manor, took over.

Ernest Lake had been employed by the old Sidmouth Water Company which was then owned by the Lord of the Manor, Colonel Balfour, and his Estate Manager was Major Hastings. It appears that Mr Scadding, who worked in the Sidmouth Manor Offices, was promoted to Water Manager. They always said it was because he was a freemason. To me, he was the most inefficient bloke, as I eventually found out in later years.

When I first went there Mr Scadding was as nice as pie to me and I done what he asked me. The first time I clashed with him and found out he had a bit of a temper was after about a fortnight.

Another part of my job was to go over to the corner of Glen Road and Manor Road every night about six o'clock. I used to leave a stop-cock key in the hedge there by Glenholme. I had to turn on the two stop-cocks at that junction to boost the water supply because they were running short of water at the Redlands Hotel during the night due to the demand. The hotel at that time was owned by Mr Pickard, who was also the Clerk of the Council.

In Manor Road there was a 3" main and in Glen Road there was a 5" and 3" mains both coming from Peak Hill Reservoir but there's a branch of the 3" main that supplies as far over as Connaught Gardens in Manor Road where the Redlands Hotel was.

Anyway, Mr Scadding decided to connect the 3" main and the 5" main together with some 1½" lead-pipe. He'd given me all the equipment and stop-cocks and allowed me about half-an-hour to do the work. There was one, two, three, four, five, six, seven, eight, eight joints to wipe, 1½" joints with a blow-lamp and all hand-done, you know. The joints had to be prepared, scrapped, tinned, the brass fittings on the stop-cocks had to be all clean. In-fact, it took me over two and a half to three hours.

Mr Scadding came tearing back to the office, which was also where our workshop was back at Woolcombe Lane, and yelled at me, 'What the hell are you doing? How much longer are you going to be?'

Peter Lake was there and he said, 'What the hell do you expect, Gerald's got eight joints to wipe there. You don't know anything about it.'

Mr Scadding was frightened that Mr Pickard would make a complaint about him

That was my first entanglement with Mr Scadding. I didn't answer him back or anything because he just flared at me, 'How much blooming longer,' you know, 'What the hell you doing?'

He didn't know anything about the job. He'd been in the Manor Office, and that's the first time I found Scadding would shout and rave when things didn't go right. And what was the point of a 5" main which has been fed from Peak Hill reservoir and a 3" main from Peak Hill reservoir? You ain't giving it anymore pressure! You might be increasing the flow a bit, but you ain't increasing no head of water because it's coming from the same reservoir. It used to improve it a shade, in regards to quantity, but it didn't improve the pressure at all. It didn't make any difference at all because they were both coming from the same heads of water and your pressure is determined by your heads of water. But that was what I had to do.

He didn't know what he was talking about, he had no experience or that, he'd only been in an office. Peter Lake stood up for me because Peter didn't like him much, but that was my first encounter with him. I found out later that Mr Scadding was called Amos by several local plumbers because they thought his decisions were influenced by the moon!

Anyway, my loan to the Sidmouth Water Department lasted six weeks. To me it was completely different from my previous plumbing work but I really enjoyed it, going round checking for leaks or things that they wanted me to do.

Quite often he would say to me things like, 'Well, you can go home this afternoon and have a rest, but I want you to go out in the night about six o'clock and go looking for people using hosepipes!'

I used to go home and read a good book or something. I had dinner with my father, and then go in the front room, pull the curtains and lay up for the afternoon and I'd get the tea ready, and this went on continuous for the six weeks I was on loan to the Council.

One day during these six weeks the Water Department had a major problem at Woolbrook reservoir, which supplied the bulk of the town. No matter how much water they pumped from the bore hole at Sidford the water level in the reservoir couldn't be sustained.

Anyway, Vera and I were out courting one night and I took her for a walk up round Mutters Moor and down through the golf links. We had a kiss and a cuddle on a few seats on the way and then I walked her home to Manstone.

Just as we came through Manstone past 'Big-Bum Churchill's Corner' towards the junction of the main road I heard a hell of a noise of rushing water.

I thought, 'What the devil's this?'

I went and looked and there was water pouring everywhere and running into a gulley at the side of the road. I took Vera home, kissed her good night and that was that for day.

When I went to work the next morning I said to Peter Lake, who was the foreman, 'You know, I was out with my girlfriend.'

'You and your girlfriend,' he said, 'You're always out with her. I hope you're walking a straight line?' he said.

'Of course I am,' I said, 'and I tell you what Peter, we came through Manstone past 'Big-Bum Churchill's Corner' until you come to the main drag and on the right hand corner there was water going like hell!'

Of course, he went and told Scadding who jumped in his car, he had a Standard, a grey one with a union-jack on the bonnet, Standard something anyway, and told Peter Lake and me to jump in the car and take him and show him where's to.

Anyway, I took them over and showed them where to and that was the leak that was losing the water at Woolbrook reservoir.

We only had two labourers on the Water Department in them days, and they borrowed a chap from the Sidmouth Gas Works, because we had no mechanical tools at all. All we had was a pick and shovel, a sledgehammer and gad. That's all we had, we had no mechanical tools but the Gas people had what was known as a 'warsop'. It was a mechanical digger and 'Ticker' Pinney and our own two labourers, Freddie Salter and Toby Hawkins, dug their way down through the concrete, which took several days, using the 'warsop.' They dug it all out and found a 4" main with a 1½" circumferential cut break.

I had never came across that word until years later, when our chief engineer at the East Devon Water Board, Mr Eric Gordon, did the monthly reports. He always referred to breaks as either circumferential or longitudinal, for example; we repaired 18 circumferential cut, breaks or factures and 22 longitudinals.

On another occasion, within the next week, I was going to work for the water department in Woolcombe Lane and I saw water running in Mill Street, at the end where the old prison was, into a gulley. It had broke the surface of the road, so I told Freddie Salter and Toby Hawkins and they went down there and found the leak.

So whether this was because I showed an interest or no, after six weeks I left Sidmouth Water Department and they thanked me for what I'd done and they said that if ever there was a job came up, which there might possibly be, would I be interested?

And I said, 'Yes I would consider it.'

Chapter Fourteen: A Welsh Wedding

A Welsh Wedding

A Life in Sidmouth

I spent six enjoyable weeks with Sidmouth Water Department and after that was finished I went back to my old firm of F T Dunn in Temple Street to carry on my employment there.

I can still remember, quite distinctly, Mr Dunn saying to me, 'I've got a job for you at Southerton.'

Southerton is a hamlet in Newton Poppleford. The job was to 'plumb-in' and install a complete new hot water system for Mr and Mrs Jack Berry who ran a small-holding there. Mr Berry, I well remember as a child, used to work in the Co-Op delivering bread to peoples houses. He married a Miss Gooding who used to live in Lonely Cottage down the back of 'Taxi' Hodges and Whitton's the butchers. They had quite a large family and when I went out there it was rather hard to begin with. I used to go out by bus every morning and walk up to the end of Southerton and the same in the evening.

Dunnsfords was relations of theirs and they were re-doing part of the house and I had to put in a new hot water system. But the funny thing was that there was no water there because Southerton came under Newton Poppleford which in those days was administered by St Thomas's Rural District Council and the water supply hadn't been brought there.

Anyway I was there several weeks and completed the job, tank in the loft, general new hot water system, everything, but when it was finished, to test it all, they, the Berrys', had to pump water up from their well in the garden by hand, fill up buckets with the help of one or two of the other members that were working for Dunnsfords, and pour the water into the tank in the roof so I could test the system. I suppose I was there about three weeks.

In the meantime, Vera and I still continued meeting and carrying on our courtship and then she said to me one day, 'I'm going home next week. I've got a week's holiday from Woolworths. Would you like to come home and meet my parents?'

I said, 'Yes, but I can't come immediately.'

A Welsh Wedding

So Vera went home on the following Saturday and I went into Exeter with her to Exeter St David's Station, and four days later I set off for Cardiff to join her.

I hadn't been there before and Vera met me on Cardiff station on the Wednesday. She give me a kiss and a big hug and was glad to see me and we changed platforms and caught the train for the Rhondda Valley which took us right up to her home town of Treherbert which is at the end of the Rhondda Valley.

I remember I had a small case with necessary things in, clothes and so forth, and we walked from the Treherbert station, up Station Road, across Bute Street and up to Vera's home.

I felt there were eyes looking at me and I said to her, 'That lady is looking out her shop there!'

Vera said, 'That's Mrs Millard the Milk.'

And after a while I found out that in Wales everybody is referred to by their trade or profession. There was Millard the Milk, Thomas the Butcher, Corfield the Butcher, Johns the Shoe and Richards the Undertaker.

Vera's parent's lived in 135 Dumfries Street, Treherbert. Vera opened the door and we went in. It was a terraced house in a row of miners' cottages and on entering the passageway I remember there were ordinary 6" tiles with a floral pattern and highly polished.

I met Vera's mother, Celia, who was in the kitchen. There was a range in the kitchen where they boiled their water. There was no central heating, no bathroom or anything. Vera's mother had lunch ready. I believe, if I remember rightly, she had pork chops with lovely cauliflower, cabbage and roast potatoes and apple pie was the desert.

Her father, Frederick, was still at work at that time, but he came home later, I think it was somewhere about six o'clock. As I mentioned previously, he was a 'banksman' at the Glen Rhondda Colliery. Because there was no bathroom they used to boil the water on the old range and the man of the house would wash himself in a hip bath. But the thing that impressed me more than anything, was that, looking round the house you'd never think it was a miner's cottage because everything was spick and span. There wasn't a bit of dust or anything.

And another thing I found out later was that if you worked in the mines you were allowed a free delivery of coal, which I believe was about a ton or two ton a month, but it wasn't delivered in sacks like we was used to in Sidmouth. No, a lorry came along and tipped it up in the back lane and Vera's father would carry it in and store it in his little outhouse. When you looked in this outhouse down at the bottom of the garden where the toilet was, the big lumps of steam coal was all put round the edges as if you were building a house, and all the smaller coal was tipped inside. It was kept immaculate.

Anyway, I met her parents and we got on well. Her mother had a sense of humour. She always used to laugh at most things I said and the day went well.

I think in the evening we went up to meet Vera's sister Gwen and her husband. He lived further up the road and had part of a house which belonged to Gwen's father and mother-in-law. His name was Hayden Fairchild. He was a foreman in the colliery at Treorchy and he was a big man.

Well that was the first day. It went quick and I slept in what was the little back bedroom, which was nice and cosy. Vera's father had just changed shifts and he had to go back on the night shift.

The next day came and Vera took me round to meet her relations. I met Vera's older sister Nellie who lived about three miles further up in Tynewydd at Bryn Wyndham Terrace. She had three boys and a girl. Her husband, Reg Snell, drove the engine that let the men down the mines in the cages to the bottom of the pit.

A Welsh Wedding

The next day we went out through the Rhondda. Vera took me down on the bus to Treorchy and in the afternoon we made various visits to some of her relations. Her mother's from that area though Vera's father had come from Langport in Somerset where he lived with his parents. The family had left Langport during the agricultural depression and moved briefly to Australia but returned to Langport. Vera's father moved to South Wales to work in the coal fields.

Anyway the next three or four days were spent acquainting myself with mid-Wales. We walked up what to them was the New Road, and looked away to the north to Brecon. The New Road takes you right over the top of the mountain down to the other side to what is known as the Head Of The Valleys Road. We were invited to Vera's cousins for tea one afternoon. Again, coal-miners, and again, the house was just glistening, shining, it really impressed me.

We stayed until Saturday and then we came back together.

I always remember I had left some money in an envelope for my stay there on my dressing table in the bedroom which I slept in, but four days afterwards the envelope and money came back to me. Inside was a note saying that they were only too glad to have me and Vera together on holiday. I always remember that.

Anyway, I came back and I went back to work for Dunns and this continued up until February. In the meantime Vera and I carried on our courtship as usual. We still went and saw the band, went to pictures on Saturday, we went out somewhere on a Sunday, had coffee somewhere, and we went on long walks.

On Fridays Vera used to go to choir practice at what was then the Congregational Church, now the United Reform Church. Vera did have a lot of friends in Sidmouth, many of whom I got to know as time went on. They often invited her out to tea on a day off and that's how I got to meet Mr Barber and his wife.

Mr Barber was the Superintendent at the Norman Lockyer Observatory in Sidmouth. They lived at Lamacraft in Manor Road.

A Life in Sidmouth

Mr Barber was an only child and his father lived in Salcombe Road in a house called Carberry.

Vera also went to church on Sundays.

Anyway, this went on and then my father said, 'Would Vera like to come to lunch one Sunday?'

So Vera came to lunch and after that, it became a regular thing every Sunday. She also always came back on a Saturday night if we'd been to the pictures or somewhere and we'd have fish and chips for supper.

I think it was the second week of December 1948 that I wrote to Vera's parents and asked them if we could get married, and I had a letter back by return of post saying they were delighted and they welcomed me into their family.

We're coming up now to Christmas and I was still working for F T Dunns the plumbers carrying on my normal employment and Vera carried on hers at Woolworths.

We finally decided we would like to get married in February 1949 so Vera came and stayed at the house with father and I over the Christmas, and after Christmas, I think it was about the second week of January, she gave up her job in Woolworths. She gave her notice in because we were going to get married and we settled on the date being the 19 February 1949.

One thing did annoy me at the time though.

I was brought up in the Church of England. I'd been to church most Sunday mornings, I went to Sunday School every Sunday afternoon, and when I got older I went to bible-class on Sunday afternoons. But when I went to get my Banns called at the Parish Church in Sidmouth to get married, which is the normal thing to do, and Vera got hers called in her Baptist Chapel back home, the vicar

A Welsh Wedding

came round to me and said he couldn't call our Banns because Vera was a Welsh Baptist and they didn't recognize that as a religion.

I lost practically a days pay and had to cycle up to Honiton and have our Banns put outside the Registry Office there.

Anyway, my father was delighted at the news we were getting married. He took to Vera, very, very well. They got on like a house on fire and we were married on the 19 February 1949.

I went back to Treherbert two days before this to help with preparations. My father came up on the Friday night, the day before my wedding, with Maurice Hart and his son. Friday was an atrocious day, weather-wise. Irene, one of my twin sisters, came up from Kent with her husband Ted and their son David for the wedding, as did many of Vera's relations. Her sister and brother-in-law was there, her other sisters with their children and several cousins also came.

We were married in the morning about 10.30am at Blaencwm Baptist Chapel in Treherbert, and the wedding reception was held at Vera's house at 135 Dumfries Street. I don't know how they crammed everyone in.

I remember we had a sit down dinner, and I also recall that the cars for the wedding were supplied by a Mr Hughes who lived near Pontypridd. He had a taxi and undertaking business. Vera had apparently met Mr and Mrs Hughes when they came to Sidmouth on holiday and went to the Eagle Restaurant where she worked at the time, and he always told her if she got married he would supply the cars. They took to her I think, you know.

Vera and I had a week's honeymoon at my sister Irene's home in Dartford, Kent.

Chapter Fifteen: SUDC Water Department

SUDC Water Department

In the meantime, I had a letter from the Council offering me a permanent job with the Sidmouth Water Department as a Water Inspector, which I accepted, and I started my life with them on, I think it was, the 9 March 1949. I think my pay was £3 something a week.

It was totally different to what I was used to. I lived in Mill Street and the Water Manager Bert Scadding lived in a house called Umtali in Millford Road, now the Willow Bridge Guest House. He later moved next door to Westdene. The procedure was that I used to go to him at quarter to eight in the morning. From there I went up to measure the levels of Peak Hill Reservoir and do any other jobs that he wanted me to do. After this I went home to breakfast and then back to Mr Scadiing for nine o'clock.

As a Water Inspector, I started at the sea-front going round house to house checking for leaks and consumer facilities and this was checked against the Sidmouth Urban District Council's ratings.

No-one had done this for years. I had note books, which I've now donated to the Sidmouth Museum, and I recorded each house I went to; the name of the person, if they were in and the number of baths and 'wc's' they had, and also if they had an outside tap.

Under the old rating system you were allowed one bath and one 'wc' under the General Rate. If you had two baths you paid 10/- a year extra, and if you had an extra 'wc' you paid an extra 10/- a year, which, when one looks back at the water-rate today, was peanuts.

I can't be 100% certain but I'm almost sure that the water rate for the town in 1949 was eleven pence ha'penny (11½d) and I think the SUDC Water Department made a small profit.

Anyway, I made these records as I went round and then on a Saturday morning I'd go and see Peter Wallis, the Rating Clerk, who kept the Rate Book, to exchange what I'd done that week, and if he found that someone had, for example, more wc's than listed they'd automatically be charged another 10/- when the next Rate was due. This went on continually and was the main aspect of my job.

Going up to Peak Hill Reservoir every day became very irksome to me as did another job I had to do on Saturdays and Sundays when I had to go to the pumping station at Sidford. There were two bore-holes there, situated down at the bottom of the playing fields. There was a big 'treble-ram' pump that had to be oiled and also some was bottles that had to be topped up with oil. To me, personally, after a few weeks, and thinking about it, I thought it was nothing else but a farce.

I thought it was one thing to keeping me on the go, and this is why I began to see what Mr Scadding was really like.

Gerry Pike, who was the foreman, and I had to go up to Sidford every Sunday at ten o'clock in the morning, twelve o'clock, two o'clock, four o'clock and six o'clock to see that the oil was dripping on to the mechanical and moving parts of the 'treble-ram' pump. The two bore-holes that were there, pump the water from Sidford to Woolbrook Reservoir.

You have to remember that the Sidmouth water undertaking back in those days got most of the water from springs.

At Sidford there was a 5" and 7" mains that came down from Sidbury that were fed from springs up in the valleys above the village of Sidbury at Horseshoe Plantation, Ousley-Goyle, Wolversleigh-Goyle and they all eventually, via various tanks and catchment areas, ran into these mains pipes that came on all the way down through there. There was also another spring from Virkin's Well. These were well up in the valley of Sidbury.

I understood that these were brought down in the late 1800s because the Sidmouth Manor, under Colonel Balfour, owned the land up in that area at the time but was sold off when he died.

But that's how the water came down to Sidmouth, it was practically all spring water and it was very, very soft. And all the water in the town came from there which fed the main intakes to Peak Hill Reservoir and Woolbrook Reservoir. The other main supply was the springs across the golf-links.

Anyway, Vera and I moved into our family home which was 16 Mill Street, where my father resided, and we looked after him. And then in September, late September 1949, Susan came along, our first little girl.

This is again where I found that Scadding wasn't the man I thought he was, and in fact was a difficult man to get on with. He wouldn't give me any time to come home to look after Vera and the baby. He wouldn't give me any time off at all. I gradually found him to be a real tyrant. And this behaviour towards me continued, I suppose, until November 1962 when Mr Scadding was taken ill. I still continued to go to his house and get instructions for the day's work that he wanted done and I got the impression that Mrs Scadding was as capable as him at running the Water Department.

Here's another thing that comes into my head. When Mr Scadding did eventually die that month, we still continued to go to Mrs Scadding to get our orders. This went on until Bond & Finnimore, two local plumbers, said to Gerry Pike, our foreman, 'We want to install a water connection to a new building.'

Gerry Pike replied, 'I'll have to see Mrs Scadding!'

Gussie Bond, who was also the fire officer at the time, said, 'What the hell do we have to go and see her for?'

I understand that Gussie Bond went and saw the surveyor and wanted to know what the hell was going on? Mr Scadding had died about five weeks previously and there was Gerry Pike, the foreman, and me getting orders from Mrs Scadding! So anyway, after that, a stop was put to it.

I found Mr Scadding, who on appearance was a very nice chap, to be a bit of a tyrant underneath and most inefficient.

We clashed many times and on occasions we didn't speak. And then, Peter Lake, who worked in Tavistock, came up one day and saw me. I was at the point of having a nervous breakdown because of the way I was being treated by Mr Scadding. I was working every Saturday and every Sunday. It might have been only for a few hours but I wasn't paid any overtime.

What happened was, I'd got into a bit of a state and I was going to throw the job up.

I did have a word with my old friend Harvey Culverwell who owned the Sidmouth Herald and he said, 'I wouldn't do anything yet Gerald, sit tight!'

So anyway, I bumped into Peter Lake one day who always came to see me and he said, 'What's the hell's the matter?'

I said, 'Honestly I can't put up with this much longer. I've been working every day. I was even going on a coach trip one day and he came down and said someone had complained about chlorine in the water up at Cotmaton Road, and would I go up. And I told him I was going on a coach trip and he said that was too bad and I lost my coach trip.'

Anyway, Peter Lake bumped into Ted Pinney whom he knew very well. Ted was one of the family of F Pinney & Sons the builders and also Chairman of the Council at the time. Peter Lake came back after talking to Ted and told me to go up to Ted's house and see him. I went and saw Ted at 9 Barrington Mead, Sidmouth. I went and saw him and he told me to make an appointment for me to go and see him one evening out of hours, which I did.

I told Ted Pinney about the first time Bert Scadding and I clashed. I had a bicycle which belonged to the Council, I had no other means of getting round, carrying my stethoscope, water keys and things for turning the water off.

I told Ted that Mr Scadding said to me, 'What's the bag you've got on your bike?'

And I told him my reply was, 'Well, that's my bee-keeping gear. When I finish work at five o'clock, I usually call in and look at me bees.'

To which Bert retorted, 'Well, you can stop that!'

I told Ted about several other incidents I'd had with Mr Scadding, like I later found out he was frightened of Councillors, and after another clash with Mr Scadding, I said, 'Well, next time I see Edwin Hill, the Chairman, I'm going to have a word with him and ask him if this was right?'

The next morning Mr Scadding said to me, 'We'll forget about the thing carrying the bag on your bike.'

Another time I was playing tennis at the Coburg Fields and Mr Scadding said to me, 'Were you playing tennis last evening at Coburg Fields?'

To which I replied, 'Yes, I play every Monday and Wednesday from five-thirty after my tea.'

Scadding declared, 'I want you to stop playing tennis because the Councillors will think you're not working!

I told Ted about his attitude towards me, like he didn't speak to me for days on end and that, and also about the hours I worked and what not and I said 'I've never had a day off, only when I go on Holiday and there's always a fuss when I have my fortnight's holiday.'

Ted said he couldn't do anything about Scadding's attitude to me, but he said, 'Leave it to me.'

General Witham was on the Council at the time with two other Councillors and what I understand happened was that Ted brought the matter up at a special Establishment Committee Meeting. Ted said he had seen Gerald Counter going up Peak Hill Reservoir every Sunday morning and General Witham wanted to see all the Water Department time sheets and this is what happened, and there was nothing on them about this Saturday and Sunday working.

Gerry Pike and I were told by Scadding not to log it down as it was irrelevant. During the summer months I had to be up Peak Hill by 6am and every night at 7:45pm to start up a pump which was at the bottom of the golf-links drive. This pump boosted the water supply into Peak Hill Reservoir but in so doing it sucked the water from the higher levels at the top of Bickwell Valley and Peaslands Road. Anyway, this all interfered with my social life as I couldn't do anything else during that time.

So on the day they had this Establishment Committee Meeting I was going up to Peak Hill Reservoir on my bicycle and I had got as far as Fourways when I saw Mr Scadding parked there in his car.

'Jump in Gerald,' he said, 'I'll give you a lift up to the pumps.'

So I jumped in and we went up and started the pumps and on the way down he stopped at Fourways where I had left my bicycle, and then he asked, 'Do you belong to a trades union?'

I said, 'Yes I do.'

And then he said, 'For your information I've had a very uncomfortable two hours this afternoon,' he said, 'at the Establishments Committee Meeting.'

Mr Scadding was in a hell of a tear. This was the beginning of the end of our working Saturdays and Sundays all the time. The Council,

160

at a General Meeting, declared that the Water Department Inspector and Foreman, had to have every other Sunday off, and we were going to be paid for it. The payment we never had but in the end we worked two and had one off.

That was the downfall of Mr Scadding and through that I found out that he was afraid of the Councillors.

Another of my jobs for the Water Department was, that if we had heavy rain, I had to tear up to the golf-links and go right across them to Nut-Tree Plantation, where all the springs were, because the water on the golf-links used to get discoloured with heavy rain. I never found it all that discoloured but this is what Mr Scadding made me do; I had to go up there on my bicycle. I've been up there in thunderstorms at two or three o'clock in the morning. I've gone across there in the middle of the night putting wooden plugs into the tanks to stop the discoloured water going down to Peak Hill Reservoir.

Anyway, as I said, I found out that Mr Scadding was afraid of the Councillors.

He said to me one morning, after a terrible thunderstorm during the night, in a very sharp tone, 'Did you go up the golf-links last night?'

'Yes I did, to put the plugs in,' I said, 'and I bumped into Councillor Pinney.'

'What the hell was he doing up there?' he said.

I replied, 'Well, I think he plays golf now doesn't he?' and went on, 'Ted asked me what the hell I was doing up there at that time of night? And I told him it was part of my job to go round and put plugs in the water tanks to stop water getting back into Peak Hill Reservoir.'

That's all I said to Scadding.

I never had to do that job again, he stopped me doing it. It seemed he just liked to keep everybody on the go. He used to go to Sidford pumps himself in the morning, at six o'clock, in his car. There was no need for it.

He went home to dinner at half past twelve, one o'clock, and he never came out again till five o'clock, he was home every afternoon. His idea was that he was resting up because he went up the pumps early in the morning. But that's the sort of bloke I was dealing with.

Anyway, I said to Ted Pinney, 'I was thinking of giving up the job!'

He said, 'Don't do that, the SUDC Water Department will be taken over by the East Devon Water Board eventually.'

So I stayed and stuck it out. Mr Scadding died in '62, I'm certain it was November 1962, and the East Devon Water Board took over in 1964.

In the days of the SUDC Water Department the water supply would be turned off in some part of the town between 2pm and 4pm every Thursday for maintenance work. In those days, we didn't do repairs on stop-cocks in the road; the consumer had to get their own plumber to do it. What happened was this. We'd arrange to do so many stop-cocks in an area. The consumers would get it dug up in the morning all ready and prepared, and I would shut the water off at two o'clock till four o'clock to enable them to get all the repairs done.

My job was, for example, if the main town was going to be turned off, I started at nine o'clock in the morning at the top of the town at Sidmouth Dairies, and went down through Temple Street and called in to all the relevant premises in the town; restaurants, cafés, hairdresser, barbers and hotels, and notify them that the water would be off from two o'clock till four.

I often got a lot of back-chat from the hairdressers. I remember going up 58 Temple Street to Norman Cook's hairdressing salon, and he created hell.

A Life in Sidmouth

He was a cockney from London, and he said, 'What the hell do you mean you're gonna shut the water off?'

I said, 'Well, that's the procedure sir. That's what we do every Thursday.'

If anyone ever criticised me I always remained polite and under control. I never back answered anybody back.

And Norman said, 'What do you mean hairdressers?'

I said, 'Well, I tell all the hairdressers.'

'We're no hairdressers!' he said, 'Do you realise I come from London? We're the only real hairdressers in the town!'

Generally though, I built up a relationship with people in my job and I took the attitude all the time to always remember when you're dealing with people, it don't matter who they are, whether it's the Lord of the Manor, or whether it's the person in the Council house, they all got feelings, and that's one of the things that always stuck in my mind.

Another thing I always thought to myself was that if I only learnt another word for my vocabulary, I've learned something during that day or that week.

And I suppose, over that period I got to know, well, everybody in the town certainly. I went in everybody's house checking for leaks and I knew practically all the trades people and enjoyed a good relationship with them.

I remember one occasion which stands out in my mind. I had to go and see Mr Tracy, who was a manager of the South West Electricity Board (SWEB) shop. He wanted his outside stop-cock repaired and so I arranged to do it one Thursday afternoon.

I don't know whether it was because he was dealing with Mr Tracy in the electric, but Mr Scadding said, 'No, we won't do it this week, we'll do it next week!'

So I had to go round and see Mr Tracy, who was a very efficient but very outspoken man. And I always remember I was there talking to him with his under manager, George Brockington, and there was a gentleman sat in a car there, outside the electric showrooms, and he lit up a cigarette and threw the empty packet out of the window.

Mr Tracy went over, picked it up and said, 'This is yours sir!'

The man in the car replied, 'No, I don't want it!'

And Mr Tracy retorted, 'No, and nor do we want it!' and threw it back in his car.

I had several bad experiences when we had the water restrictions on. One of my jobs was to go round in the evenings from about 7 o'clock to find people that were using hosepipes or sprinklers and report them.

Anyway, one thing that did disillusion me and help form my opinions about life in general and my attitude to society was this;

Mrs Campbell-Watson, who was quite an influential person in the town, lived at Powys. I saw she had six hosepipes going, watering some trees, Cedar of Lebanon, if I remember rightly. Anyway, I made an appointment to see her within 24 hours, which was procedure if I was to make a complaint, and I agreed to see her one afternoon at 2 o'clock. I went there about two minutes to two, rang the doorbell and the servant came, there were several servants there. The servant showed me into the hall where I stood from 2 o'clock until a quarter past three, when Mrs Campbell-Watson came out of the drawing room and into another room and just ignored me.

Then, at quarter past three she sent for me and I went in to see her.

I said, 'Good afternoon madam, I'm from the Sidmouth Water Department, and I must tell you what the water restrictions are. You've got six hosepipes laid down, watering your trees which is not allowed.'

'Be off with you! Rubbish!' she said, 'I'll use whatever water I want to!' (or words to that effect).

So I just left. I didn't argue with her at all.

So the following morning when I went to Mr Scadding to report he said, 'Where the hell were you yesterday afternoon? What were you doing?'

I said, 'Well, I done some routine inspections, and then I had an appointment to see Mrs Campbell-Watson because she had six hosepipes laid out watering trees, and as you know I go out every other evening looking for hosepipes and sprinklers because of the restrictions.'

'Well,' he said, 'keep away from Mrs Campbell-Watson. I had the chairman of the Water Committee on the phone last night for 20 minutes. Forget about Mrs Campbell-Watson, she's been very good for the town, she gave them a shrub to go in the Goyle in Manor Road!

Another time I went to Mr Blanchard, the surveyor, who lived at a house called Redgates in Manstone Lane. I was working that area checking for leaks and doing inspections on toilets and baths and I discovered that Mr Blanchard had an outside tap which was chargeable at 10/- a half-year, and so I noted it in my Water Inspection book.

The system was, every Saturday I took my Water Inspection book to Peter Wallis who was the Ratings Officer at the Council. Peter Wallis, who had the most beautiful handwriting you could wish to see, was an elderly gentleman, and he kept the Rate Book.

Anyway, I saw Peter and told him I'd found an outside tap at Mr Blanchard's and asked him to see if he was paying for it, which was £1 per year (10/- per half year).

And Peter said, 'No, he isn't!'

So he must have been sent a bill for another £1 per year.

Anyway, I think it was on the following Wednesday, Mr Scadding said, 'Where the hell were you last week?

I told him, 'I was up at Manstone Lane.'

'Well,' he said, 'I believe you. I've had a lot of ear-ache from Mr Blanchard. He said he's got an outside tap and he's got to pay a pound a year for it.'

'Well, that's what you told me when I took this job on, that any extras I've got to report it.'

And Mr Scadding said, 'Well, in future keep away from Mr Blanchard, give him a wide berth.'

He was frightened, and this is what I found out, he was frightened of anybody that would stand up to him.

Here is another incident that occurred during the water restrictions. I think it must have been about 1958-9 and there was about 19" of water remaining in Peak Hill Reservoir and there was a gentleman who lived in Cotlands Estate, the second house in on the right hand side. Vosper he was called, Mr Vosper. He was from up north.

Anyway, his lawn was immaculate. It was laid with Cumberland turf, one of the most expensive turfs you can have. I went up the reservoir on a Sunday morning to check the levels and low and behold, Mr Vosper had two sprinklers going. I'd been and seen him on two occasions before and had cautioned him.

I was never aggressive when I cautioned anybody and my method of approach was always, 'Good morning sir,' or 'good morning madam.'

On this occasion I came back from the reservoir which only had 19" left in there. So I went to see Mr Vosper and knocked on his front door that was ajar. The building was constructed in an 'L-shape.' Out came Mr Vosper.

I said to him, 'Good morning sir. Actually, I have been to see you twice before about your sprinklers,' I said. 'You're affecting the water supply and we only have low levels in the reservoir. And on top of that,' which we were, 'we are having complaints at the top of Cotlands that their pressure is falling.'

He didn't answer me. He turned around and went behind the front door and pulled out a gun, a revolver sort of gun.

He put some, which I take it must have been bullets, in there, and he stuck it in me tummy and said, 'If you don't get out, I'll blast you out!'

So I walked backwards down the pathway, got on my bicycle and went home and thought about this.

Anyway, on Monday morning I saw Mr Scadding, after all he was the boss, and he agreed to come with me to see Mr Vosper at this bungalow. We went up there, it must have been about half-past ten in the morning and I knocked on the door and introduced ourselves to him.

I said, 'Good morning sir. This is my engineer, the water manager Mr Scadding.'

Mr Vosper ignored me.

He turned immediately to Mr Scadding and said, 'I can deal with you sir,' he said, 'but I can't deal with this chap, he's got the most vile, filthy language I've ever heard in my life! He abused my wife yesterday with his filthy language.'

I'd never seen his wife in my life, never seen her. I'd always seen Mr Vosper, I didn't even know what she looked like.

Mr Vosper just desecrated me in front of Mr Scadding, and all that Mr Scadding could said was, 'Leave that to me sir, I'll deal with it.'

And then we left.

The gentleman that lived next door was Mr Marsden, who I knew, not as a friend or anything but because I used to chat with him when I saw him fly-fishing. About mid-morning, Mr Marsden, came down to see my wife and knocked on the door at 16 Mill Street.

He said to Vera, 'Tell Gerald that I heard everything that took place yesterday and if there's any problem with his job I will stand up for him. I heard everything he said on Sunday morning and Monday morning, so tell him not worry, I will vouch for what he said.'

Anyway in the meantime, I went to see the Clerk of the Council, who at that time was Mr Howarth. Somebody told me I should have gone to the police, someone drawing a gun on you like that, but anyway I went to the Clerk of the Council.

Mr Howarth response was, 'Well, it's best not to make a fuss Gerald because it would be bad publicity for the town.'

That's as far as I got. That's a true story that is!

I had many clashes with Mr Scadding but in the end it was apparent that he was frightened of various Councillors and anyone else who would stand up to him.

On Thursdays, also as part of my job, I used to go to Mr Scadding's house at about a quarter to twelve and he'd give me the pay sheet with my name, Gerry Pike, no he was paid monthly, I was paid weekly, Freddie Salter, Toby Hawkins and Jim Perry.

Jim Perry, who lived in Salcombe Road, worked for the Water Department part-time. He was in his seventies then and used to do the water chlorination. In the old days, the water chlorination was very primitive. Jim would go off early in the morning about six o'clock or half-past six, go to Woolbrook Reservoir, then Stintway Reservoir in Stintway Lane, which is only a very small reservoir, and then he'd walk across the golf-links to Peak Hill Reservoir. And what it was, he'd have a 50 gallon barrel at each reservoir, which he used to get from Mr Spiller at Burscombe Farm in Sidford, that was filled with water and a certain amount of chlorus that was put in to purify the water, and at the bottom of the barrel there was a wooden tap and a piece of tubing going into the reservoir. That's how primitive it was. And he would set the drip.

Jim would fill the barrel with a rotary pump, pump it up out of the reservoir, filled the barrel up and then he would put in a quantity of chlorus, that was predetermined, and it was dripped into the reservoir and this was done each time he went there in the morning and each evening between six and eight o'clock. He would also take a sample of water out of the reservoir each time he went there and test it to see what the amount of chlorination was, usually it was about 0.2.

To add to the tale there was a lady in Broughton's one day talking about Jim and the quality of the water. Now Jim was a teetotaller and a decent sort of bloke. He was very old fashioned and always wore a 'dickie-bow' tie funnily enough. I used to think he was a prominent freemason when I knew him as a kid.

Anyway, Vera was in Broughton's and over heard the conversation.

This lady was complaining about the taste in the water these days, and she says, 'Off course, this old boy who does it, trouble is,' she said, ' he goes down the pub drinking night times and he forgets how much he puts in, he chucks it in by the bucketful!'

Which is completely not Jim's character, he didn't drink, he was as straight as a die. If he'd heard that he would have gone spare!

Anyway, back to the pay sheet saga. Bert Scadding would give me the pay sheet and I would go down to Barclays Bank, get the pay, and then I had to take it back to him, and he would put it in envelopes.

And then one day I went down there, this was after a couple, three years, and he said, 'By the way, they under paid you down Barclays last week by two shillings and nine pence!'

I remember this as though it was yesterday.

'Well', I said, 'I can't go down now Mr Scadding.'

'Yes you can,' he said. 'Go back and tell them when you take the money down today!'

So I went back and I said to the clerk at the bank, 'My employer, my boss, said that he was short changed the other week.'

'Well,' he said, 'he should have raised it then, not now. Sorry,' he said, 'but I can't do anything about it now Mr Counter.'

Mr Scadding was a most peculiar man, he was. He would pick on me all year round and then at Christmas time he would give me a box of chocolates for Vera.

My girls, Susan and Olwen, used to go over and see Mrs Scadding at Christmas and she'd give them a tin of sweets each, but I found Mr Scadding most peculiar.

On another occasion, I'd been on loan to Sidbury Manor to do some work. Early morning and late night they had some trouble with one of their supplies, so Sir Charles Cave borrowed me from the Council to do some night work up there to see if I could find where the water was going, which I did eventually help him to overcome his problems successfully. That was in; I believe that was in the August 1957. I thought no more about this, Sir Charles Cave thanked me for what I'd done personally and that was it.

Three months later, I was home at lunch, and he sent one of his employees down to me, with an invitation to come to The Court Leet Annual Dinner, which was held at The Royal Oak in Sidbury.

The Court Leet is an old system dating back to about 1400, and part of their custom was they used to have a dinner. It's when I think they set the rents for the farmers and tenant farmers.

Anyway, I thought out of courtesy I'd better tell Mr Scadding that I'd been invited.

And I did, I think it was after lunch one day when I went over there, I said to him, 'By the way,' I said, 'Sir Charles Cave has invited me to The Court Leet Annual Dinner at the Royal Oak next Thursday.'

And he didn't know anything about it, but he said to me, 'Oh yes, I knew all about that. He rung me up and asked my permission so he could write to you!'

What a load of old rubbish. I think his wife must have had a hell of a life with him!

Another time I got called by Mr Scadding and he said to me, 'Go up to Enslie in Cheese Lane.' I think the house was called Enslie, but I can't be sure of that. 'We've had some complaints. The people up there said we've been poisoning them!'

So I went there about eleven-thirty, twelve o'clock. The house was split into two flats. I knocked and a very elderly lady came to the door.

I said, 'Good morning madam,' I said, 'I believe you've had some trouble with the water supply?'

'Yes,' she said. 'You're poisoning us!"

I inquired, 'How do you mean exactly, other people are having the same supply? Can I come up and see what the problem is?'

So up I went up these stairs and she took me into the kitchen where she drew some water in a glass. I didn't want to drink it because the glass looked a bit grubby.

She said, 'It's horrible. It smells, and when you boil it,' she said, 'there's all scum on it.'

'I can't believe that madam," I said.

So she went and got a saucepan and said, 'We'll try it out.'

Well, when you boil water in a saucepan, vigorously, you get bubbles don't you, like scum.

So I said, 'Get me a table-spoon,' and of course I drew it off and it went back to normal.

Minutes before this happened there was a groaning noise, this is true, coming from down the passage, 'They're poisoning me! They're killing me!'

She said, 'That's my brother,' and out of the toilet, which he'd just used, came an old boy about seventy or eighty.

'That's my brother!' she said, 'He's got the same problem. Look at him!'

And true as I'm here, if you imagine that doorway, there was an old man seventy or eighty, standing in the architrave of the door with his feet wide apart and his testicles and his whatsit all hanging down, and he had a pair of red socks on. It's funny what you remember, it's my wicked sense of humour. Anyway, she made me go up to him, and she made him turn round in front of me, and he was covered in sores, terrible sores.

Well, it was revolting! And the stench from him, and the stench from the toilet, whether he had flushed it or no I don't know, but it stinked and that!

She said, 'There, this is what your water's doing. Look at it, it's disgusting! I want something done about it!'

I said, 'Look madam, I don't think it's anything to do with the water,' I said, 'but I can arrange for our chemist to come and see you,' that was the procedure, 'or,' I said, 'your doctor?'

Anyway she went and got some cabbage to boil and of course you still had this froth on it but when you put the spoon in it cleared but she wouldn't accept it. They were hell-bent that we were poisoning them. So I went back and reported to Mr Scadding and I think, I'm not sure, the Medical Officer of Health got involved. Anyway, the old boy died six weeks afterwards. I did ask about it and apparently they were both suffering from malnutrition.

I continued on the Water Department until there was talk in the press about Water Boards were being formed. There was the North Devon Water Board and there was the East Devon Water Board and there was a South Devon Water Board and there was talk Sidmouth, Exmouth and Exeter were outside of these organisations, and it was very political, they didn't want to become involved with the Water Boards, but eventually there was an Act made and Sidmouth, Exmouth and Exeter were taken into the East Devon Water Board.

But before that happened Mr Scadding had died and Peter Lake, who had lost Sidmouth originally in Christmas 1948, and went to Tavistock as the Water Engineer for the North Devon Water Board, came back to Sidmouth as our Water Engineer.

But when I look back, and I used to say so at the time, if Peter Lake hadn't come back here, or if the East Devon Water Board hadn't come in, I think the Sidmouth water undertaking would have collapsed round our ear-holes, I was convinced of that.

During the period I worked for Mr Scadding, nothing was ever done, apart from my waste detection, looking after the pumps and various other jobs as I have mentioned, but he never done anything constructive. He never improved the system and he never spent any money on the infrastructure of the water undertaking whatsoever. Well, they did, in 1960-61, sink a new bore-hole at Two-Bridges, Sidford, in the field below there known as No 3 Bore-Hole, and they built a new reservoir at Core Hill.

Most people said the Core Hill reservoir should have been higher up but I think myself, that what lay behind the Council's thinking was, that they were afraid they were going to get development up the sides of the hills further because our supply was limited because it was a gravity supply.

This was why the Council was so much against the Water Boards coming in to spend money to improve the supply, and I think if we had stayed as we were with Mr Scadding the Engineer the old system would have collapsed.

We never had a van until late, about 1959, and the labourers used to have a wheel-barrow. If there was a leak; I remember on one occasion there was a leak outside Vallance's Brewery in Temple Street and the labourers walked there with a wheel-barrow and pick and shovel and hammer and gag. They never had any mechanical tools. They dug it all by hand and repaired the leaks.

I remember Mr Gordon, Eric Gordon, the Chief Engineer for the East Devon Water Board, he came down to meet us in our Office about six or seven months before this take-over.

Our office, by the way, had moved from Woolcombe Lane, because they built flats there, our Office had moved to Sidford in Byes Lane. They built offices there for us, and a store.

Anyway, Mr Gordon came down to meet the staff. There was our two labourers, Toby Hawkins and Freddie Salter, Gerry Pike, myself and Mr Scadding.

I remember Mr Gordon said to me, 'What do you think Gerald, of being taken over?'

And I said 'Well I think, personally sir that it's inevitable and we've gotta move with the times. It's no good looking back, and there are things that want improving.'

Whether that impressed him, my answer, I don't know, but after that when we eventually got took over I got on very well with him. I thought he was a very good engineer. He was a very good advocate, he always seemed to be able to go to the Ministry and get money for new projects and that. I got the impression that he was quite a progressive gentleman and that.

SUDC Water Department

Chapter Sixteen: East Devon Water Board

East Devon Water Board

A Life in Sidmouth

The East Devon Water Board took over in 1964 and not long afterwards Mr Gordon said to me, 'Are your salaries weekly paid?

And I said 'Yes.'

And he asked me, 'Would you like to go on the permanent staff?'

I replied, 'Well yes.'

Actually I was, and this is true, I was promised by the Sidmouth Urban District Council, which I took it up with them, that I would eventually be on their Superannuation Scheme, but they never did. I asked Bert Scadding about it twice but he never done anything about it.

Anyway, Mr Gordon said to me one day, 'Would you like to be superannuation and be paid monthly Gerald and go on the staff?'

And I said, 'Yes sir.'

He said, 'You'll have to have a medical.'

So I went and had a medical with the East Devon Medical Officer of Health and he passed me as very fit. So Mr Gordon took it up at the Establishments Meeting of the East Devon Water Board and I eventually became a member of the staff on their Superannuation Scheme.

I'd been with the SUDC for fifteen years and I'd never had any superannuation, but Mr Gordon negotiated on my behalf and got me 15 years back superannuation. He was very good to me and I got on with him. Some people didn't like him but he was fair to me and I gave him my all. I told him that you gotta accept change and that I liked my job and you've just gotta move with the times. I think that impressed him rather than this dog in the manger attitude, you can't do anything about it like, you know.

East Devon Water Board

I always remember the first thing Mr Gordon said to me, 'What method of transport have you got?'

I said, 'I've only got a bicycle.'

And he said, 'We'll have to get you a van.'

And from there on I never looked back.

Peter Lake carried on as Water Engineer, but he clashed with the East Devon Water Board. I could never understand this because Peter always argued that when you get the Water Board in, you get all the equipment, all the pneumatic drills and everything, and he was all for it, but yet, for some reason, he clashed with them.

This used to embarrass me and I was very, very friendly with Peter, very, very friendly, and I told him when he came back as Water Engineer I'd give him my all, which I did. I supported him as he had forgotten a lot, when he came back, about the old system in the town, and he relied on me for things like, 'Where do you shut this off?' and, 'Where do shut that off?' like you know.

I remember that Peter, I always referred to him as Mr Lake when anybody of any consequence was there, to me that was the right thing to do, was often rude to Mr Gordon when he came by our office.

Mr Gordon lived at Exmouth and often used to call into our Sidford office on his way to the EDWB HQ at Honiton.

He would talk to us about things but Peter would always say something like, 'Well, don't ask me, ask Gerald. He knows more about it than I do!'

This used to embarrass me a bit and I think this was one of the things Peter did wrong, and after that Peter was sort of, not crucified, but they took him away from Sidmouth and I ran the supply for several years. They took Peter and put him at Honiton. They sort of humiliated him and put him in a lesser responsible job like, you know.

And eventually they moved him from Honiton and he had to go in the office at Exeter doing menial tasks. But I'm sure it was only because he clashed with them.

We had a man called Howard Pendelbury, you might have heard of him, he had a photographic mind. At one time Peter had a clip of 5 dead cartridge shells stuck on the window sill and Mr Pendelbury saw this and reported him and Peter had to dispose of them.

Another time he had one of my tobacco tins with a candle inside with a little note saying, 'Emergency Lighting,' and during a visit by Mr Gordon and the deputy engineer Jack Taylor, somebody said, 'Who's the comedian?'

And Peter said, 'Well, I am, like the rest of you!'

He was having a knock at the East Devon Water Board, and to me, it wasn't the right thing to say. Peter was an intelligent man but I think Peter wanted a more senior job, but because he clashed with them, I think, they did, they demoted him, there's no doubt about that, and poor old Peter, he ended up with stomach cancer, and after he went to Exeter, he went down and down like, you know.

But I kept in contact with him and used to take his wife to visit him, not every night but most nights. I was very loyal to him. He looked after me. He came back to Sidmouth and treated me like a human being, unlike Mr Scadding.

I think it was 1971 they moved Peter Lake to Exeter and I was left in charge in Sidmouth to run the area. I came under the Honiton area but I was left to my own devices but overseen by the Superintendent at Honiton, who was Reg Foxwell.

He was a very nice chap, very quiet. He came down to see me and spent the morning with me. I told him I'd give him every co-operation, the same as I had given to Mr Lake and that.

181

But he said, 'You know more about the area than I do Gerald and I shan't interfere much.'

I was thrown in the deep end. My first major works was to employ gangs of men and lay mains around two new estates in Sidford, which were the Green Close area and Malden Road, which was developed by Broseley Homes.

I was in charge of a couple of gangs of men and we laid 100mm pipes all round both estates. That was the first job I had running the area on my own. I had two labourers of my own in Sidmouth who did the general maintenance, but it was an eye-opener to me because under the old SUDC Water Department Mr Scadding never done anything like that.

Going back to when Peter Lake was in charge, there was another kerfuffle when Peter Lake came back because the old SUDC Water Department had just laid mains round an estate and he wanted to know where the money was coming from for funding it.

This caused a bit of a fuss locally amongst some of the builders and developers because, apparently, when you laid infrastructure around an estate for a developer, they had to contribute towards the cost, but the cost generally returned as each house was developed so much was knocked-off the cost of development.

I remember one or two of the local builders came and created hell. They had to pay a deposit before the mains were laid. They had to contribute towards the cost of it. I could see afterwards, I wasn't involved in this sort of thing, but what had previously been happening was that the Council had been laying mains round the estates and the rate-payers were paying for them to the benefit of the developers.

So when Peter Lake came back he took this up with the Council and they had to contribute towards the cost of laying what today we would call the infrastructure I suppose. There was quite a fuss about that.

A Life in Sidmouth

Anyway, I was sort of thrown in at the deep end and I ran the area, I suppose, for about five years on my own. If there was a major job on I would draw labour from the Honiton area, where the head quarters of the original East Devon Water Board was.

Mr Gordon built new offices for me at Sidford No 3 Bore-Hole, which was sunk in 1961, just off Two-Bridges Road opposite the Police Station. Prior to this our original offices with the SUDC Water Department were at Woolcombe Lane, and when flats were built there we moved to Byes Lane Pumping Station in Sidford.

There was talk at one time that Mr Gordon was going to build two houses there, one for me and one for my labourers who came from Honiton. The idea never materialised but Mr Gordon was very keen on it.

So I had new offices and stores at Sidford, and he had a garage put up there for the van and our equipment. I was responsible for all the stores and that. He always used to come, about once a year, and check everything.

I had to do the administrative side, keep all the records of what pipe and what materials was used. I was involved in doing the chaps time-sheets and sending them to Exeter every week.

I was also responsible for the main pumping station at Sidford and three little sub-stations, and eventually as we became more involved with the EDWB they laid a new 10" main from Sidford to Branscombe Tower.

They took the main across the river and through Harcombe Fields, up over Trow Hill till you come to the junction with Old Trow Hill and then they diverted the 10" main up through Old Trow and then along the right hand side of the road towards what is now known as Branscombe Tower which eventually would push water on to Seaton and Lyme Regis.

But I saw more work and things happening with the EDWB than I saw in the 15 years I spent with Mr Scadding. The EDWB laid a new trunk main; a new main that picked up the end of the main outside the cemetery gates; and we laid a new 9" trunk main right down through the town to the seafront to boost pressure and demand.

Mr Gordon spent a hell of a lot of money. The EDWB also had wash-outs put on the ends of roads for flushing, so we could flush the mains out. They also installed fire-hydrants.

Nothing was done in Scadding's time, the Council's time, they never spent anything.

When Unwins built Core Hill reservoir for the SUDC Water Department that was the be all and end all of everything. There was more work done in the two years under the EDWB than in the forty-two years I spent in the water industry. Mr Gordon was a very progressive engineer, there's no doubt about it, he had a lot of fore-sight and that.

Mr Gordon also sent me on courses. I went to Blagdon near Bristol, Bristol Water Works, on courses on water detection. I went to Ewell in Surrey on a course all to improve your knowledge of the water industry. And another place I went to, I went there twice, was near Goring-on-Thames.

The East Devon Water Board made a lot of progress in Sidmouth, improvements to the supply and distribution in the town, and to the reservoirs.

I remember we went to Peak Hill Reservoir. It took us three days to gradually empty it down. Mr Gordon wanted to inspect it to see what condition the concrete lining was in. The reservoir holds three quarters of a million gallons of water. We washed it out. It took us exactly one night. Mr Gordon came about midnight and we went in the reservoir to see what it was like inside it. It was in a pretty poor state. He arranged for work to be done in there but eventually the reservoirs were done away with.

A Life in Sidmouth

What we done, we took the water from Core Hill. I'm not sure about this, but I'm 90% certain, we know Peak Hill Reservoir's gone and I understand Woolbrook Reservoir's gone. They're taking water from Core Hill and it's going straight into the supply, they bypassed the reservoir at Peak Hill and they bypassed the reservoir at Woolbrook, so there's only one reservoir, Core Hill, as far as I know, now in use.

After a period of time we became South West Water and then South West Water was privatised by Mrs Thatcher. I remember going to London on a protest meeting against that, I think we went to Westminster Hall or Conway Hall.

I'd finished with the water. I eventually retired after 42 years. I enjoyed my job. There were ups and downs with the consumers but I always managed to take care of it in the end.

I took early retirement at 63 rather than stay to 65.

I thought I was going to miss my colleagues and that when I retired, but I didn't. I thought I was really going to miss people, but I didn't. I had my bee-keeping and I suppose Vera and I had a more relaxed life.

Vera was glad I retired.

Vera thought I was going to stay until I was 65 and was more than surprised when I came home one day and said, 'I'm gonna finish!'

And she replied, 'Never!'

I said, 'Yes, I've written a letter in asking for retirement.'

East Devon Water Board

Chapter Seventeen: Early Retirement

Early Retirement

A Life in Sidmouth

I took early retirement because I could see what was happening. Things were getting bigger and I thought the personal touch was going to go and I believed in personal contact with the consumer.

There was a meeting called by South West Water PLC to discuss the take-over. There were about 150 of us there. The new management of South West Water PLC, I can't remember what he was called, Chris somebody, but he was introduced to the meeting and he got up and gave a speech and started to talk about how we would deal with consumers.

Mr Peter Howarth, who was our area manager at the time, got up and said, 'There are three members of staff here with over 41 years experience and I'm sure they don't need a lecture about how to deal with the public. They've dealt with them for over 40 years!'

This meeting was on a Tuesday and by Friday midday Peter was gone!

We always thought this was rather sinister. He got the poke. We always thought, because he got up at that meeting and spoke up for us, that was the beginning of the end.

Peter Howarth did alright for himself though. I believe he went to Severn Trent Water and he must have received a good redundancy payment, severance pay and that. He then he left Severn Trent Water and was with another water company when he retired.

Peter Howarth was a good manager. He was what I refer to as a man's man. In fact it was through him that Vera and I received an invitation to the Queen's Garden Party at Buckingham Palace on Tuesday 11 July 1989 (4-6pm). He was asked to recommend someone from the grass-roots level and he recommended me because of all the good work I had done over the years.

I had a retirement do in Exeter where there's always been a bit of nonsense and leg-pulling about Sidmouth.

Early Retirement

I went to the Exmouth office for 3½ to 4 years when I was with the South West Water PLC from the Sidford Office and when Exmouth closed down I moved back to Sidmouth and then Honiton which is where I retired from.

Anyway, there was always a bit of leg-pulling. Sidmouth always got the money. Ted Pinney was Chairman on the SUDC. His heart was in the town and he always got more money for Sidmouth. Sidmouth got money for their Britain in Bloom business and this used to wind up the Exmouth chaps.

We got comments like, 'When you go to Sidmouth there's more people out there doing the gardens than there is anywhere else in East Devon.'

There's always been a jealousy of Sidmouth from all the neighbouring towns like Buddleigh Salterton, Exmouth and Honiton. I've always felt that.

When Ted Pinney went, I always thought that was the beginning of the end of his influence, because he was a good councillor. He might not have been popular but most times I think Ted was a good councillor for Sidmouth.

During the course of my working life I kept many documents relating to my water inspection days and the seemingly ever changing developments relating to Sidmouth's water supply and maintenance, including the original Government Act. I have donated these Water Inspection Books to the Sidmouth Museum along with my father's original Rent Books for 16 Mill Street and other associated material. Images of one or two of these documents are reproduced in this book.

Chapter Eighteen: Allotments and Pastimes

Allotments and Pastimes

A Life in Sidmouth

During the early part of our marriage, up until about 1970, I had two allotments up at Salcombe Hill. We grew our own vegetables. My father had one allotment and then I took on another one and I ran two allotments. This was when I was keeping bees the same time.

I used to hand-dig one allotment and a chap called Charlie Chick ploughed the other one out every year. He used to come from Manstone, from his nursery there. It cost me £2.50 to have one allotment ploughed, which was dirt-cheap I thought. He had to load up his tractor, come all the way down to Salcombe Hill from Manstone, he used to plough it for me and he used to plough it deep, it weren't no, one of these rotovators, it was a proper plough, and he ploughed it and then I used to knock it back rough.

He ploughed it in the autumn for me and I grew potatoes in one and vegetables in the other; cabbages, broccoli sprouts. We were practically self-sufficient regards vegetables. I'd go up there after I finished work and go up on weekends and cultivate the two allotments. I never went Sunday afternoons.

Sunday afternoons were spent with the family. We went off for long walks. On several occasions we went up Peak Hill and walked into Otterton.

My father was living then, so this was before 1966. We used to leave dinner for my father and Vera and I would get a BBQ chicken or something and we would take our lunch and tea along with us.

We'd go from home, up Peak Hill, down into Otterton, go in the King's Arms pub at Otterton and buy a bottle of beer, two bottles of lemonade for the girls and a bottle of Babychamp for Vera and we'd walk down beside the River Otter and sink it in the river. That was our fridge.

We'd have our lunch and then walk on into Buddleigh Salterton. Sometimes, we walked back the other side of the river from down at Buddleigh, go over the bridge, come back through what's known as

Otterton Park back to Otterton, and then back through Ladram and home again. Sometimes we'd catch the bus home from Buddleigh, depending how we felt.

Another of our favourite walks that Vera, the girls and I did, was to get a bus to Beer and then walk up over the cliffs and all the way back to Sidmouth.

I remember on one occasion, we'd walked all the way from Beer and we'd just got to the top of Trow Hill, when Mr Carnell, who owned the Woolbrook Garage in Woolbrook, came along in his car and asked, 'Do you want a lift home Gerald?'

The girls wanted to get in the car but I replied, 'No, we've walked this far so we'll walk the rest of it!'

So we walked down over Trow Hill, by which time it was six or seven o'clock, and we called in at the 'Blue Ball' and had a beer and lemonade in the garden. We then walked down through The Byes and all the way home.

Another walk was to catch a bus to the 'Hare & Hounds' and then we walked along Chime Way, then we'd cut along East Hill Ridge and then cut down just above Fire Beacon. Again we had a picnic lunch, BBQ chicken or something.

I remember once, we went in a field there and had our lunch. Just then a young chap called Peter Gooding came in and said, 'Here! That's my father's field, bugger-off out of there!'

The four of us sat there having our tea and didn't take any notice of him. We eventually walked from there down Fire Beacon Lane, came out by the 'Bowd Inn' and caught the bus home. We were absolutely shattered that day.

We used to do a lot of walking on Sundays, perhaps that's why I'm worn out now, I don't know.

A Life in Sidmouth

Vera had a friend who was a nanny. Her name was June Hillman and she was from Buddleigh Salterton. She was the nanny to Mr and Mrs Meek who owned the Marlborough Hotel. Vera got to know them when Susan and Olwen were small. I think Olwen was about six at the time.

June Hillman used to go to Mousehole in Cornwall for her holiday with her sister I believe. Anyway, Vera decided, we were going to have a holiday as we hadn't been on a one before, other than to Vera's parents, usually at Easter when the singing festival 'Gymanfa Ganu' was on, and again after Christmas.

It was always a bother asking Bert Scadding for my holiday time. He always had some moan and groan about it and that.

Anyway, this was around 1964, Vera said, 'We're going to have a break, we've always gone to my parents. We'll go down to Mousehole!'

Vera's friend June told her that it was no good her going to Mousehole because she didn't have a car! The thing is there is no transport down there. Anyway, we booked up to go.

In Sidmouth there was a shop called Timothy Whites and the manager was Mr Tonkin from Newlyn. He said that his parents took people in for Bed and Breakfast. If we were going down there to take a cottage in Mousehole, we could go to his parents B&B on a Friday night.

So Vera went into Exeter and booked for us to go by Royal Blue which used to run a service to Penzance in those days. We left Exeter, the first time we went at a quarter past five, and we got to Wherry Flats off Alexandra Road which was where the Royal Blue bus station was in Penzance.

Mr Tonkin asked his parents and they said that they would put us up for Bed & Breakfast for Friday night till we went to Mousehole on the Saturday morning.

Allotments and Pastimes

Well, it was an experience to go and stay at the Tonkin's.

We arrived there at a quarter past ten at the bus station. Mr Tonkin was there waiting for us to carry our cases and that to his B&B which was about half a mile from the bus station. So we walked to Mr Tonkin's residence in Newlyn Road.

By the way, that's the lady who painted the picture for us of Mousehole harbour. She was a wonderful artist, not trained or anything, purely an amateur artist. She used to do these paintings and put them in the front window and sell them. Cost me £5.00 that one.

Anyway, we got to Mrs Tonkin's and she said, 'I don't expect you've had anything to eat.'

This overnight stop became a regular thing thereafter until I had a 'Standard 8' motorcar in 1966. I bought the car for £50 but after 12 months I had to have a new 'Gold Seal' engine fitted by Peter Barnes the mechanic at Ted Andrews Garage on the Esplanade in Sidmouth. It cost me £46-0s-11d. We would go to Mrs Tonkin's, stay there Friday night, after we went by Royal Blue.

Twice, Edwin, a friend of ours from Branscombe said, 'I'll take you down, if you want to, in my Morris 1000.'

By this time I had a scooter. I didn't go into work on the Friday, so Susan and I went down to Mousehole on the scooter in the morning. We done it, I think, twice. And Edwin would bring down Vera and Olwen and he would get down there about ten o'clock and on each occasion when we went to Mrs Tonkin's at ten o'clock there was an evening meal waiting for us.

Well, you'd have a shock if you saw that, I've never seen anything like it! Two big fat pork chops, roasted with the skin on, crackling all on, cauliflower or broccoli, three or four roast potatoes each, this was ten o'clock in the night, and there was always suede and lovely gravy, but it was nearly always pork chops.

A Life in Sidmouth

Edwin, our Morris 1000 friend, would stop and have a meal, and then he would turn round and drive right back home to Branscombe.

After the main course there'd be usually, peaches, tinned peaches, sliced peaches or else apple crumble with a load of Cornish clotted cream.

We done this for about six years running until I got a car in 1966 but Mrs Tonkin was a wonderful, wonderful cook. And we always went, when we were down on holiday, we always went back and saw her. She would always invite us in for a bit of a snack with them for tea, and when we went in, there was always pasties for the girls, me and Vera.

Mr and Mrs Tonkin's were very pleasant people. He was a fisherman. He had a boat, a trawler, which belonged to Shippam's the meat paste people at Chichester. During the pilchard season he went out with two other colleagues fishing for Shippam's, but the rest of the year the boat was his to use as he wanted to.

I remember the first night we stayed there, we got up in the morning and Mrs Tonkin's said to me, 'Mr Counter, do you like fish?'

I said, 'Yeah, I eats everything Mrs Tonkin!'

Well I was amazed; I'd never seen anything like it. I had a whole 'brill,' which is a type of flat fish like a plaice, laid on a plate for breakfast. It was, I'm not kidding, it was as big as that foolscap paper, and it hanged down over the plate.

She said, 'Do you mind having a few chips with it?'

I said, 'No.'

This was for breakfast (*Gerald starts laughing*) at half past eight in the morning. Then there was tea, bread and butter, toast and marmalade afterwards, and cereal and that (*still laughing*). I shall never forget that.

Allotments and Pastimes

Vera said, 'You're never gonna eat that!'

I said, 'Not much. Of course I'm gonna eat it!"

Vera and the girls had a cooked breakfast, but I ate this plaice, this whole brill. You see brill down in the shops at Buddleigh, they're all speckled, a little bit like a plaice, but very brown.

We became friends with the Tonkins and we always went there. Then after a time we had a car. This was by the time my father died in 1966. We had a 'Standard 8', so we used to drive to Newlyn then ourselves. We didn't stay at the Tonkin's then. We would go straight down there on a Saturday and make a day of it.

We all went to Cornwall, Mousehole and Penzance, for about forty-six years. We were creatures of habit.

And then one day I got it in my head that I was going to walk from North Wales to South Wales via Offa's Dyke, which is a well know footpath in Wales. I was going to hitch-hike from Sidmouth to North Wales and then do this walk on me own.

My father said, 'Talk's cheap!'

That's what he said. Anyway, I never got round to this walking but we suddenly decided that we would go over to Builth Wells for our holiday as a break from Cornwall.

So I worked out an itinerary. It was going to take me about four days to get to Builth Wells. Susan by this time had left home. She was in commerce. She'd got older and that and had her own friends, so it was just Vera, Olwen and me. Anyway, we left early in the morning thinking it was going to take four days to get there! Well, we was over the Seventh Bridge and in Monmouth by about twelve o'clock!

We had a coffee in Monmouth and a look round the town, which was very old, and then we drove from there up to Ross-on-Wye which is about half an hour away. We had a look round Ross-on-Wye, had a snack there, and from Ross-on-Wye we went to Hereford.

Hereford was a bit frightening to me. By this time I had a Morris 1100, and I remember when we drove into Hereford, about six 'mods' on scooters got either side of the car and they were shaking fists and allsorts as we drove into Hereford. Luckily, I shook them off and we went into Hereford, which was a very, very busy town. We stopped there and had tea, and after a time finally made our way to Builth Wells.

I was overcome by the scenery. The scenery was absolutely fantastic. We went down through what is known as Golden Valley which brings you down to Hay-on-Wye and eventually to Builth. We went to the tourist information place and they sent us to a house at Llanelwedd.

Anyway, we went to the house and Vera looked at the mat in the porch and said, 'I don't fancy going in there, they haven't swept the front for weeks!'

She didn't like the look of it.

Anyway, we went in and knocked on the door and a lady came and I said, 'We're looking for accommodation. The tourist board sent us here.'

She said, 'I'm sorry, I can't take you. I'm going to the south tomorrow, but I've got a friend I can recommend.'

So we went to a place called Llanfair Guest House which was the other side of the river near the Groe Car Park in Builth Wells. Anyway, we went there and knocked on the door and a lady came, a Mrs Cockham. She said she had some vacancies and there was a nice car park at the front of the house, which apparently had previously been a doctor's residence.

A couple of years afterwards while we were there, like we always done wherever we went we walked around the villages, we came back one night and met an old boy leaning out over his gate. We started up a conversation, you know I'm a chatterbox, about the place. He'd lived there all his life.

He asked, 'Where are you staying?'

I said, 'We're staying with Mrs Cockham at Llanfair.'

'Oh," he said, 'I don't know if you know,' he said, 'that's the last house that Dr Crippen lived in before he set sail to leave the country!'

And one or two people have told me that since but I've seen no official words though.

Anyway, the only trouble was that Mrs Cockham didn't do an evening meal, so she recommended a pub in the town called 'The Black Ox,' an old 'drovers' pub.

Anyway, we went there but weren't very happy with it. The following day was Sunday and we went out for a nice drive all up round Rhayader and the lakes and reservoirs. We then started thinking about what we going to do for an evening meal. We found a pub called 'The Swan' and we went inside.

The proprietor was Mr Price.

I said, 'We're looking for somewhere to get an evening meal.'

He said, 'Where are you staying?'

I said, 'We're staying with Mrs Cockham at Llanfair.'

'Well,' he said, 'it's a bit late, it's eight o'clock, but if you'd like to come back at half past eight,' he said, 'we had a football dinner here last night,' he said, 'I'll see if my wife can rustle something up for you.'

'Well, we would like something,' I said, 'because it's my daughter's, it's Olwen's eighteenth birthday.'

So we went back at half past eight.

There were flowers on the table, a little card for Olwen wishing her a happy birthday and we had a fantastic meal there, absolutely fantastic.

We found out later that Mr and Mrs Price had worked at the Mullion Hotel in Cornwall. He was the head waiter there and she was the chef., and through conversation, we found out that he knew Harold Wilson who used to come there and stay with Montague L Meyer. Harold Wilson was an economic advisor to Montague Meyer who was a timber importer.

Anyway, we had such a wonderful meal there. I asked, 'Can we come back tomorrow night?'

And we went back every night for that week and then we, this continued for a couple of years and every time we went to Builth we went to Mr Price at 'The Swan' for our evening meal.

Then one day Isaid, 'See you next year Mr Price.'

'Oh, I'm sorry,' he said, 'we're leaving.'

So, we had a chat about this and he gave me the impression that he was leaving the area, like, you know.

So I said, 'Oh we're disappointed.'

But next year when we went, we found that Mr Price had bought 'The Lion Hotel' in Builth, which was quite a big place but very drab from outside.

Apparently a young couple had owned it but had let it run down. The young couple also owned a certain amount of fishing rights on the River Wye in the town, but when they sold the hotel they sold the fishing rights off to someone else, so, unfortunately, Mr Price didn't own any fishing rights.

But we went to Mr Price for our evening meal at 'The Lion Hotel' and I can honestly say we've never had food like it. There was always Herefordshire beef and their duck was a speciality. We lived like Kings and Queens there to be honest. We went there every night and they looked after us.

We used to go in about half an hour before our meal and go in the bar. We got to know quite a few of the locals, like Artie Morgan. He was a 'Linksman' on the road. It was his job to keep the gullies and ditches cleared and open. Then we got friendly with another chap who was always there, Keith Powell. He was a dustcart man. We also got to know Mr Jones. He was a Councillor and I used to pull his leg something shameful and that. And there was Mr Williams a retired Bank Manager, he used to be in and they used to look forward to us going in there.

Keith had quite a good voice. He was in the choir in the church and he and Vera used to sing 'Sweet Beulah La' which was a Welsh song about the village of Beulah. They used to sing that some nights, 'Come on let's have a song.'

Oh, our evening meal, it amazed me. We used to wonder how Mr Price made a living because we were about the only people what was ever in the restaurant.

We went in the restaurant, blooming great room, well heated and that, and Mr Price was a perfectionist. His table was laid up and he used to wait table. Mrs Price was the chef, and then Rosemary, the eldest daughter, they had two daughters, Rosemary trained as a chef at Hereford College, I think. But the food there was truly amazing.

A Life in Sidmouth

For all we ate, the meal cost us about £3.50 to £4.50 each, whatever, don't matter what you had there. There was always usually soup to start with, good home-made soup, there was the main course, desert afterwards, which was banana splits and 'knickerbocker glory.' You only had to ask for it and they'd turn it out for you. Then after that there was always cheese and biscuits and coffee afterwards.

I don't know how he done it for the price especially as there was very few people there. Very rarely, on two occasions, there was another chap, funny enough, that came from South Devon. He'd been down to Carmarthen to the cattle markets buying cattle. We met him on a couple of occasions, but I found out afterwards, that most of Mr Price's money was made doing lots of functions there, like weddings, things for the police, and I think the Masonic used to have their dinners there. But the food was truly outstanding. I can't say anything else about it.

In fact when we came to have our 40th Wedding Anniversary we decided we was going to go to 'The Lion Hotel' with Susan and her husband, our grand-daughter and that from Gloucester and a couple of friends that we met like Mr and Mrs Price and their daughter. By this time we'd left Mrs Cockham where we used to stay.

We wanted to go to the Royal Welsh Show in Builth, it was like the Sidmouth Folk Festival, but it was booked up year on year. People would book it, before they left one year for the next year, and I rang around all over the place to get accommodation and then one day I found an address and telephone number in the Welsh Tourist Board of a farm called 'Tysa Isfaf.'

Anyway I found this number for this farm about eight miles out from Builth, and I called and asked if they could take us all for the Royal Welsh Show for a week. They said they were very sorry but they were booked up.

They were booked up for nearly a year, but she said, 'I got a friend that might be able to accommodate you.' She said, 'I'll give you the phone number, the name's Stevens.'

That's where those flowers came from (flowers in Geralds room at Holmesley).

She continued, 'She might be able to help you out, but don't ring till after half past four.'

So I rang this number after half past four, and sure enough a little voice came on, not very Welsh, and I said I was looking for accommodation for the Royal Welsh Show.

'Oh yes,' she said, 'I can take you.'

I asked if she did bed and breakfast and an evening meal, because wherever we stayed we always liked evening meals. We were never ones to go out finding places to eat.

Anyway, Mrs Stevens said, 'Yes! It's a farm,' she said, 'it's a bit out of the way, what's your name?'

I said, 'Counter.'

She said, 'It's a bit out of the way Mr Counter,' she said, 'it's about two mile up a lane up in the Begwins Hills above the village of Glasbury between Builth and Painscastle.'

Anyway, we went there and we duly arrived on the Saturday afternoon and we drove up to this farm. First place I went I drove up a bit of a cart track and ended up at an old chapel and there were two old ladies there and I asked them, 'Is this Maes-Mawr Farm?'

This was the name of Mr and Mrs Stevens farm. Roger he was called and she's called Glenys.

Anyway I always remember we went up this lane and Vera said, 'Where the hell are you going?'

I said, 'I don't know, it's further than I thought it was!'

Anyway, up the drive on the right was an old caravan, a bit of a rusty old thing, and Vera said 'I'm not staying in there!'

I said, 'Who said we've got to stay in the caravan?'

That's typical of Vera, wherever we went, if the front hadn't been shut or washed, or, what is it, 'I'm not staying in there!'

I said, 'It's a nice modern bungalow.'

Anyway, we found the farm and went and rang the front door bell and out came Mrs Stevens, a dear old lady. It was a very old farm and had been in the family for five generations. But Mr and Mrs Stevens used to live in the village and they had a bungalow built the other side of his parents farm with fantastic views over the Black Mountains and the way to Brecon and Lord Hereford's Knob. We sat in the dining room, well I don't think I've ever seen a better view than that.

We liked it so much that we stayed there for, I think, thirty five years I reckon. We're creatures of habit we were.

We went every year to the International Musical Eisteddfod at Llangollen which attracts musicians and dancers from around the world, (aka the Royal Welsh Show) and I got bitten by Wales, and I, you see, the trouble with the English is when you talk about Wales they always think of the industrial South, the coal fields, but once you get above that Heads Of The Valleys Road and Brecon and that it's fantastic scenery all up through there and they're nice homely people.

Anyway, we went there and we got on fine with Mr and Mrs Stevens and sometimes we used to pop over for a long weekend. We'd go over at Easter for three or four days.

I drove thousands of miles round Wales. I went up north, down through the Lleyn Peninsula. 'Cor, I remember we went off one day. We drove, well Olwen was with us that year but we drove, we left early in the morning and we drove right up to Oswestry and onto Llangollen, where the Welsh International Festival is held every year. Then we drove east across to Capel-Curig and along the Pass of Llanberis right on to Caernarfon Castle.

Then we went down through the Lleyn Peninula, came to Dolgellau, and we got lost there and I asked a policeman for directions.

He said, 'You wanna take the right turn further up!'

We continued on to Newtown and Llandrindod Wells and we got back to Mrs Stevens about nine o'clock at night. We'd been out since about seven in the morning.

I drove miles out there and one of my favourite trips, each time we went, was from Builth to a place called Llanidloes and then we took the mountain road to Machynlleth and from there we drove up through the Corris Valley. Why we used to love going there was they had the low flying aircraft up there training from the valley, RAF Valley in Holyhead on the Isle of Anglesey, and you could stand on the side of the road and you could see the planes going down through the valley below you, diving, fantastic.

And then we used to go out to a place called The Cross Foxes, which is between Dolgellau and Dinas-Mawddwy, beautiful scenery, down to Dinas-Mawddwy near Machynlleth. There was a big woollen mill there, Meirion Mill, and we used to go in the woollen mill which had a very small restaurant and they used to do the most delicious 'Barra Brith' which is a Welsh tea bread. We used to get 'lashings' of butter on it and that. Cor, it was delicious! Then we'd go down to the woollen mill and have a look around.

The trips all started because I was interested in the old drovers. The old drovers used to drive cattle from the Welsh markets from West Wales into Kent and London to the markets. They were important people, they brought money back into the country, and they sold the cattle. I mean, there was a place in Builth, well it was the blacksmith I suppose, but they used to shoe the cattle, and they used to shoe geese because they used to drive geese as well and they used to dip the geese's feet in hot tar and that and stick pads on the bottom to save them wearing their legs out.

But the drovers themselves were very important and from what I've read, that's been published, 'The Drovers' Roads of Wales' by Fay Godwin and Shirley Toulson, you could hear them coming from miles away, the shouting and the cattle and that like, you know. But they must have lost a considerable amount of weight driving. The BBC did a television series and talked about 'Twm Sion Cati' an outlaw-hero from Tregaron, who roamed the west and mid parts of Wales. He was like a Welsh Robin Hood, he used to attack and rob the drovers and that and take the money off them and give it to the poor. He's supposed to have existed. His hideout was a cave in Llandovery, we drove up there to find the cave.

Mr Price, he said one evening when we told him we were going to pop into Abergavenny, he said, 'Oh, which way you going?'

I said, 'We'll go from Builth and take the main road.'

'Oh, you don't want to take that way,' he said. 'Go up Capel-y-ffin.'

I said, 'Where the hell is Capel-y-ffin?'

He said, 'You go to Hay. Before you go into Hay-on-Wye, take the road on the right. 'It's quite a decent road until you get to the top. I tell you,' he said, 'I always use that road.'

'Course he was used to it. That's the only time I've been frightened.

Cor, we went up there and it was a decent road for about a mile, then we got right up the top, the scenery was fantastic but it was a one track road and I had a Renault 12 then, and, Vera was nearly in tears and I must admit I weren't far off of it. Me stomach was up in me mouth and me wheels was about 6" off the edge of this road. If you had met anything I don't know what you'd do, but we was lucky, we didn't meet anything, and the road eventually goes on for about a mile along the top and then you drop down into a valley that takes you down into Abergavenny.

Blimey! Going down this valley the road was so narrow and steep but that's the only time I admit I was frightened, Vera was nearly in tears, only I don't know what I'd have done, I wasn't much good at reversing in them days, but talk about narrow.

Anyway I saw Mr Stevens later and he asked, 'How did you get on?'

I said, 'Went on your Capel-y-ffin road but never again,' I said, 'Vera was nearly in tears!'

'Oh,' he said, 'I thought you'd enjoy the scenery up there! That's where Father Ignatius had a monastery up there down in the valley.'

A Life in Sidmouth

Gerald's Apiary at Major Clegg's property
at 'Sidleigh' in Sid Road, Sidmouth - July 1952
Image ©Gerald M Counter

L-R: John Mortimore, Mervyn Mortimore, Archie Sydenham & Gerald
Cutting a section of 'horse-chestnut' tree down in the Byes near
to 'the-cut' across to Lawn Vista to remove a bees nest (1976)
Image ©Gerald M Counter

A Life in Sidmouth

The 'Bee Man'
Gerald Counter at Radway Estate in July 2001
preparing to remove a wasps nest for Mr Smith
Image ©Gerald M Counter

Gerald's Devon Honey
Image ©Gerald M Counter

A Life in Sidmouth

Sidford Flower Show at Sidford Hall c.1973
Products (all from Gerald's Bees): Clear Honey, Honey Marmalade, Bees Wax Furniture
Cream and Polish, Granulated or Creamed Honey, Bottle of 'Mead',
Honey Walnut Fudge and Plain Honey Fudge.
Flower show was usually three weeks before the Sidmouth Folk Festival
Image ©Gerald M Counter

Gerald's Show Awards - Selection I
Image ©Gerald M Counter

Gerald's Show Awards - Selection II
Image ©Gerald M Counter

Gerald's Show Awards - Selection III
Image ©Gerald M Counter

E^IR

The Lord Chamberlain is
commanded by Her Majesty to invite

Mr. and Mrs. Gerald Counter

to a Garden Party at Buckingham Palace
on Tuesday, 11th July, 1989 from 4 to 6 p.m.

Morning Dress, Uniform or Lounge Suit

The Royal Invitation
Image ©Gerald M Counter

Vera and Gerald outside their home in Mill Street
prior to leaving for the Garden Party at
Buckingham Palace on 11 July 1989
Image ©Gerald M Counter

A Life in Sidmouth

Painting of Mousehole Harbour in Cornwall by P Tonkin
Image ©Gerald M Counter

Gerald and Vera's 50th Wedding Anniversary
at Lake Louise in Canada 1999
Image ©Gerald M Counter

Gerald Counter at Oxton House
12 September 2009
Image ©Gerald M Counter

A Life in Sidmouth

Vera, Julian King and Gerald at Holmesley Nursing Home
on Wednesday 24 April 2013
Photograph taken by Simon Horn LRPS
Image reproduced with kind permission of
©Simon Horn LRPS & The Sidmouth Herald

Chapter Nineteen: William E Coles

William E Coles

A Life in Sidmouth

William E Coles (Ben) was a real character in the town, no doubt about it. I always wished the 'Sidmouth Herald' had published an article on him because he was such a character!

Ben had worked with Ernie Bevin on Handsfords Mineral Water Carts in Bristol. He was born in Bristol and had learned a trade at Carson's Ltd chocolate factory. Some people said he was a deserter from the Army.

Anyway, he came to Sidmouth. He was an out and out socialist and he put up for the council. He advocated Sunday bowling and Sunday tennis, the courts being open, you know, which back in 1934 was like a red-rag to a bull in Sidmouth.

At election time he went round with a rosette which was literally as big as a dinner plate. On one occasion, when I think Sir Clive Morrison-Bell was the MP, George Bastin told me that he went to a meeting over the Manor Pavillion and most of the local dignitaries were sat in the front row, like Mr Fields, various Councillors and what-not, and all of a sudden Morrison-Bell said, 'Where's my friend Coles tonight?' because Coles was well-known for his heckling.

Ben Coles took 'Hansard' for every day of his life until he went back to Bristol to live with his daughter. She had a cleaning business up there. Anyway, George Bastin told me, he was there, and Ben Coles popped up on the platform and somebody shouted from the front row, he thought it was Tibby Veale, and said, 'What are you doing up there Coles?'

And Ben was very quick retorting and he said, 'Not the same as you down there touting for customers!'

Ben told me once, that when Attley (Clement Richard Attlee, 1st Earl Attlee) gave away India, he was going up the Council Chamber and Reg Pickard, who was Clerk of the Council, was on the stairs in front of him and he said, 'Ah, morning Ben,' he said, 'I see your friends have given away India!'

This is when Attley's Labour Government gave Independence to India in 1947.

And Ben, quick like a flash, said, 'You told me politics was taboo in the Council Chamber!'

He was like a flash, and there was another occasion, Rose Davies (Florence Rose Davies), she was from the South Wales Valley and was the first Labour Candidate put up here. I can't remember but Ben told me the Surveyor, L. M. Blanchard, came up to him up the Council yard, because he worked for the Council, they always said the Council give him a job, he was the Beach Inspector, to shut him up like, you know, but they'd never shut him up, and he said, 'I hope you're not supporting the lady Coles?'

And Ben replied, 'Why is it that your class of people always calls my class of people by the surname?' And he went on, 'Yes, I'm supporting her both financially and morally,' he said, and that shut him up.

Ben Coles told me this himself, he went to a meeting with Ernie Bevin in Bristol to a firm of Jewish people who had a rag-trade, and they went there because the workers were playing up because they weren't getting much money.

But the boss said to Bevin, 'Clear-off!' or something to that effect.

And Bevin retorted, 'I'll come back!' he said, 'and you'll be glad to see me yet," he said, 'before the month's out! But before I come back you'll want to get a damn good wash and a haircut!'

But he was, I suppose he was one of the most efficient Beach Inspectors we had down here, like, you know. He never got elected and he wouldn't change his politics for anything and he wouldn't put up as an independent.

I used to call in and see him on Friday, not every Friday, and he used to say Mary, his wife, she was a Sidmouth girl, Ware she was called, Mary Ware, 'Here he comes Mary,' he'd say, 'coming up here scrounging tea from old age pensioners!'

That's what he used to say (*Gerald starts laughing*).

Ben Coles lived up Arcot in a Council House. I went up there one Friday with Vera and the girls. I used to take the girls, because he had two daughters and at Christmas he used to decorate the house up fantastic with really first class decorations, which was always his tradition.

Anyway, I went this Friday and he didn't say anything, and I went up the next Friday and I said, 'What the hell's going on Ben?'

He said, 'Oh, we're leaving.'

I said, 'Leaving?'

'Yeah,' he said, 'we're going up to Bristol near my daughter Peggy. We've got older,' he said, 'and she needs us to be up near them!'

So he went up near Peggy to live but he had piles and piles of Hansard. I'd borrow them from him. He had piles and piles; he must have been stacked out by them.

I knew one local Councillor who said that if he'd got into politics he'd have made a name for himself. He was a bit of a, if you compare someone today, perhaps he was a bit outspoken, he didn't care much about anybody like.

I got to know Ben about 1949-1950. I only knew him because I was working on the Water Department and I met him doing the Beach Inspections, he had about six Summer students working with him and some of them wouldn't turn up.

I was down there one morning and Coles went for them hook, line and sinker, 'You're quite satisfied with me to pay income tax to keep you buggers in free education.'

He said they wouldn't come because they'd have to pay income tax! But he was efficient, there's no doubt about that, I mean, I know Sid Davey, he was deputy Finance Officer, and he said, 'Whatever Ben was, his politics, forget about that,' he said, 'he was efficient, and he weren't afraid of anybody.'

I told you the instance that, over where the free car parking for the disabled peoples is at the end of the beach by Clifton, where you go down the slope, he challenged a chap there who was parking because they said there was no parking.

This chap was sat there having his lunch, so Ben Coles said, 'You're not allowed to park there sir!'

And he said, 'Who said so?'

'It's a non-parking area,' he said, 'and that's from the Clerk of the Council.'

And this chap who was a traveller, took a card out of his pocket and he said, 'You go up and see your Clerk,' who was Pickard at the time, he said, 'and tell him I'm challenging his authority.'

Ben, he only had a bicycle, he went straight up the Council Offices, which was then at the bottom of Fortfield Drive, opposite there at Norton Garth, and saw Pickard who said, 'He's quite right Ben,' he said, 'we're only trying it on.'

They didn't want parking there; they were trying to keep it clear.

I told you this story, Vera was there then, and Susan and Olwen, we'd all been down for our hot-cross buns, Good Friday morning at the Bedford Arms car park and we came back via, we were opposite the York-Gap and there was two chaps there, two or three, I can't, no three I think it was, and they had cigarettes and they was burning holes in the canvas of the deck-chairs and Ben saw them.

'Look at that!' he said.

He wasn't afraid of anybody, he went straight over to them and he said, 'You can cut that out, you're damaging public property,' he said. 'Rate payers pays for them!'

And two of them stood up to Ben and said, 'If you weren't an old man who didn't have glasses on,' he said, 'I'd knock you for six!'

And Ben turned to me, took his glasses off and said, 'Hold these a minute Gerald.'

I held his glasses for him and he went up to them and they cleared off.

He was fearless like, if you know what I mean, but he was efficient. I remember as a kid there was John Mortimore, no John's brother Mervyn who's now dead, 'Chippy' Charles, Peter Weeks, and we was always prawning over Chit rocks and we'd see 'whoopee-floats.' Do you remember 'whoopee-floats?' You hired them from the Beach Inspector, they were 30p for half an hour, well 6/- in old money. They used to have them over Jacobs-Ladder and another lot by the Bedford Hotel. Perhaps there'd be ten or twelve lined up, and he'd give you a paddle. You sat on them and you had a paddle and you was allowed to go out so far with them. I remember when we had a raft chained up off the beach.

Anyway, well what we done, I went and pinched one, well not pinched one, we borrowed one, and we went and got our nets and took them out further because the tide was coming in.

Cor, blimey!, We'd been doing it for about 20 minutes and the nets was quite a way out and all of a sudden there was a voice, it was Ben Coles, 'Who the hell let you have a 'whoopee-float?' Bring it here immediately,' he said, 'else I'll ring the police!'

Cor, he had a voice like a fog-horn. I was going to go back then but I went and got the nets first then brought them in. That was the first time I suppose I met him, as a child like, you know. But he had a lot of background.

He, well, I told you about when the Rev C. K. Woollcombe spoke to him. Ben wanted work, he didn't want charity, he didn't believe in charity, he wanted work but he couldn't get any work as there was a lot of unemployment here. This was before he was a Beach Inspector in about 1933-34. He was a Beach Inspector for a long time, you know, but this was going back to early 1920s I should think.

Anyway, he was walking down through, by Sidmouth Vicarage in Vicarage Road, outside Culver House, and the Rev Woollcombe lived in Culver House and he saw Ben and a conversation took place and Ben said he didn't want charity, he wanted work, and they arranged for somebody to come and see him from the Parish Relief.

And that's when I told you they sent the two Misses Whittington from Pauntley in Cotmaton Road down to see him. They came down to see Ben who lived in, what was then, Western Town over behind the Hotel Riviera. There were quite a few houses over there.

The Misses Whittington came down and started talking, and they literally offered Ben, he showed me the letter, to pay for him and his family to emigrate to Australia. I mean, he was a bone of contention in the town I believe, if you could go back to old people they'd all tell you about Ben Coles like, you know, especially election time.

They offered to pay for him to emigrate, his wife and two children, he had two little girls then, and he said to them, because the Whittingtons' were very religious, 'If this place called heaven is such a wonderful place, why is it your class of people spends so much money on doctors bills trying to save yourself from going there?'

I know this is true because I saw the original letter. They couldn't answer it but they'd go back and consult their father.

A Life in Sidmouth

And their father wrote back, which I thought was brilliant, and told Ben that, it wasn't a lengthy letter, but it said, 'The reason they spent so much money on doctors bills is so they can stay on to save poor sinners like him from going to hell!'

But he was efficient as a Beach Inspector, no doubt about that, I think he was the best of the lot. And then in the winter they'd repair the deck-chairs. They had a place up the back of the Council Yard up at Manstone, which I think is all gone now, and they'd be up there in the Winter months, from September, varnishing them, repairing them and putting new canvas on them, and they'd all come down the sea-front in the Summer.

The first Beach Inspector's depot was where the old Sidmouth Baths was to, it was in the back of there. The old 'Baths' was between the Marine and the Devoran hotels.

Another thing he told me once, I said to him, 'Did your politics ever get you in trouble?'

He said, 'No!'

They were a poor family. Ben was a keen gardener and he kept his garden up at Arcot lovely. He told me he was down town one day with his wife Mary looking in Fields window. Now where Fields is to now, to the side where, the flower shop is, 'Whoops-a-daisy' is it? Well Fields sold furniture and Mr Coxwell was the managing director at Fields, he was a very nice gentleman, I knew him quite well, he lived up Sidbury, but later he emigrated to Australia and never come back like, and he was quite a nice chap.

But Ben was telling me he was looking in the window one day at the furniture, and you could walk down the side alley and look at the furniture through the window on the left hand side, and Mr Coxwell come out to him and said, 'What do you fancy Ben?'

It was typical of Ben, he said, 'Oh, I can't afford the prices you got in there!'

And Mr Coxwell said to him, this is what Ben told me, he said, 'Ben, I've known you a long time,' he said, 'if there's anything you want,' he said, 'you pick it out and we'll deliver it,' he said, 'and you can pay us back as and when.'

And Ben told me, 'I had a bed and a wardrobe from him and I paid him back. He trusted me,' he said, 'and I paid him back over about two years.'

Ben Coles was as straight as a die.

I remember being at our Council Yard one day. Fred Davey was the Council Foreman and Chief Fire Officer, and the siren went for a fire. The fire engine was underneath where the sports shop is now in the high street (used to be the gas showrooms, now Sports Republic). Anyway Fred Davey came out of the Offices, jumped into the van and went off like hell down to the fire like, you know.

And two of the blokes up at the Council Yard said, I was there when they said it, 'There are, Council money again, being used for the fire service.'

And Ben Coles said to them, 'Yeah, and I expect if it was your house on fire and he went on a bicycle you'd be creating like hell the other way!'

Or words to that effect like, you know. He was very, very quick, he always had an answer.

I can remember going to see him one Friday afternoon, we used to argue and debate things, and he always had the better of me.

I said to him one day, 'Cor, blimey,' this was a long time after we was married, I said, 'I've just paid my coal bill. Coal's gone up lately Ben, it's over 6/- per cwt!'

'You're right my boy,' he said. 'You'll see coal over 10/- a cwt before you're finished!'

He had terrible legs, when he was sat down he always had his legs up on a chair or a pouffe because they were swollen up, the veins and that. Whether it was trampling on the beach or what-not, you know, but he'd be as brown as a berry in no time in the summer with the wind and the weather like, you know.

But Ben was a good, I always got on alright with him, in fact his grandson wanted me to help distribute his ashes after he died. If he'd lived another three weeks he'd have been a hundred. He died down Plymouth in a home. His daughter died up in Bristol and his wife died up there, so his grandson Terry, who lived down Plymouth, he married a local girl, they had him in a home down there and that's where Ben died. Terry wanted me to go down there and help distribute his ashes but I never got round to it like, you know. But overall, whatever his politics, he also saw the other persons point of view. He wasn't narrow like, you know. He was very tolerant of other people's point of view.

Another thing he told me. At one time he worked up at Sidholme as a gardener. This was over an argument with somebody down the sea-front. He was talking politics with, 'er, oh, I know who it was, it was Douglas Dean who owned the garages on the sea-front where Trinity Court is now. And Ben said to Douglas that Mr Lindemann, who owned Sidholme, had told him, 'Your friend the big fat man,' he said, 'if he ever becomes Prime Minister he'll ruin this country (he must have been talking about Ernest Bevin) to which Ben retorted to Mr Lindemann, 'I'll live the day to see he's one of the few people who's been buried in the precincts of Westminster Abbey.' Which was an honour like, you know, and of course, Bevin was.

Ben could always remember going to the dockers enquiry when he was quite young. Bevin conducted an enquiry into the dockers, because they were in trouble. The dock owners wanted to cut their wages.

There was a QC representing the dock owners and the QC put forward what he considered was an adequate amount for a docker to live on, and Bevin arrived with a plate and he put the plate in front of the judge and said, 'Would you like to live on that?'

He had the equivalent of a day's supply of food that a docker would have like, you know, and Ben told me, 'I can remember that as though it was yesterday.'

But Ben would have been a hundred if he had lived another six weeks.

All the old people in the town knew him. He was quick to retort on anything and he weren't no fool. Whatever he was, I don't know what education he done but with regard to politics he was right on the ball, he always had an answer for everything.

He told me once that his daughter, her husband had left her, was entitled to some benefit and he wrote to the MP and to the Army authorities, because her husband was in the army originally, and she was entitled to some benefit, some payment or something, and she couldn't get it. He wrote to them and they wrote back 'pussy-footing' it like you know.

He said that unless he got an answer in a fortnight he would have the matter raised on the floor of the House of Commons, and she got her benefit within three weeks. He weren't no fool, he knew what he was talking about.

I remember another case. This didn't come from Ben, a chap called Fowler told me. The Council dug a lot of paths up Arcot but Ben, who was proud of his garden and his home, his path was done up how he wanted it, but the Council redone all the footpaths going up from the road, up the steps and they didn't do Ben's. So he got Blanchard, the Surveyor up there, and this chap Fowler worked for the Council and he knew Ben, he told me Ben borrowed a pick-axe and dug up his path and he had his done the same as everybody else like.

Chapter Twenty: Dick Longhurst

Dick Longhurst

A Life in Sidmouth

I could go on and on, there are so many people and events that have gone that I can remember.

There was the old November Flower Show which was in the old Manor Pavillion years ago. That was a damn good show in November. It was the only one in the valley in them days.

There was Sir Archibald Bodkin, he was a Public Prosecutor years ago, he lived in Sidmouth. He had a wonderful gardener, Ern Kenwood, all these names have disappeared but there again you could come up and say 'Who's interested in them?'

There was also Mrs Radford's gardener, Harry Piper, lived in a cottage at the end of the back drive from Mrs Radford's house in Sidmount that leads into Peaslands Road and Station Road.

But I must mention Dick Longhurst.

Dick Longhurst came to Sidmouth as a child with his mother and father, and I suppose he was the oldest friend I have. He was originally from Colliers Wood in South West London. To me, he was just a boy who came and stayed in the house opposite of where I lived in 16 Mill Street in the old school house. He stayed with Mrs Previs with his mother and father. His father worked for W H Smith in Colliers Wood and Dick and they used to come down every year for, I think at least a fortnight, if not three weeks every year, never missed. I expect Dick knew as much, well not as much, but he knew a lot about Sidmouth because he was interested in the place.

As boys, I suppose I was seven and Dick was eight, we used to make paper aeroplanes and throw them across Mill Street from our bedroom windows. And, if his family were going down on the beach, or going for a walk or anything, they'd often ask me if I'd like to come. Sometimes of a weekend, my parents would come and we'd walk out to Harpford Woods, and we would have tea out there and that.

Tom Searle was the woodsman, and his wife would make you tea if you wanted it. There were swings out there for kids, there were see-saws. I used to go out with Dick and his parents a lot every time he come he came to Sidmouth, and we sort of, only because he came down for three weeks, we sort of grew up together.

And, even after his father died, his father was a very heavy smoker, his mother still came to Sidmouth, and after Vera and I was married she would come down and come to our house and meet up.

She would say to Vera, 'Let's go down to Exmouth for the day,' or 'we'll pop down so and so, or we'll pop up Seaton and go down to the beach, or go out for a coffee.'

So Dick and I remained in contact. Of course the war came in 1939 and that was the end. They didn't come here during the war years.

Then, one night, Vera and I was walking past the bowling green in the church path, and that was about twelve, thirteen years ago, and I heard a voice.

I hadn't met Dick's wife. I knew he was married, but he still continued to come to Sidmouth. He didn't know where I lived and often wondered if I still lived in the cottage and that.

Anyway Vera and I heard this voice, and I swung round and said, 'Dick Longhurst!'

And I turned round and there was Dick with his wife Margaret, whom I hadn't met, and we resumed our old friendship. They were staying, they used to come down and rent a house over in Coburg Road and stay there for a fortnight. Dick and Margaret invited us round one night for coffee and snacks and we invited them back. Then eventually, I think Margaret had more influence than Dick, they wanted to come and retire down here, and they wanted to come down here to live. They were already retired and living in Cobham in Surrey.

A Life in Sidmouth

Dick and Margaret were great walkers, great bird-watchers, and we re-struck up our friendship. And eventually they went looking for property and they'd pop down for two or three days to see if they could find somewhere, and eventually they bought a house at the bottom of Redwood Road called 'Silver Trees.'

Once they'd settled in they used to come down to us one or two nights a month and we would go over there, have a glass of wine and a snack and discuss old Sidmouth and that.

Dick, Dr Richard Longhurst, was a lecturer at Chelsea College which later became part of London University. He specialised in optics and wrote a book on the subject which is still in publication. I think Margaret did tell me the other day, it's not very much but she still gets a certain amount of royalties from them. It's used more abroad than it is in this country, but that was his job, he used to lecture at one of the Polytechnics in London about optics and that.

Then suddenly Dick got like me, he was here about three or four years and he started having problems walking, something like I did, that's what began to worry me at the time, he'd shuffle round the house.

He'd never been to Exbury Gardens so we took them there one day. It's the Rothschild Estate near Southampton. Rothschild went all over the world gathering rhododendrons and azaleas, terrific they are. If you ever get the chance, go there. Anyway, we took them there for the day because they'd never been there.

Anyway, Dick developed this shuffling business, he found he couldn't move his legs properly and that. Anyway it gradually got worse. He'd had prostate cancer and been treated for it like I had, but he gradually deteriorated and in the end I used to go over and sit with him in the morning in his sun lounge. I'd make tea for him and we discussed old Sidmouth, like you and I have, because he was interested in the town, you know. He worshipped Sidmouth.

Dick gradually deteriorated in health. I used to take him out in the bath-chair. The last time I took him out I pushed him all the way along the seafront, the millennium walkway, up the 'chine' at Connaught Gardens and down past Clifton. That was the last time I took him out.

Eventually he went into hospital and gradually deteriorated over several months. I used to go every night, after we had tea at half past five, and see him up at the hospital and sit with him. Margaret would go up and help feed him and I'd bring her home in the car sometimes during the Winter. He was in hospital for about three months I suppose.

Dr. Morris used to say to me, 'You're a very loyal friend Mr Counter,' he used to say.

I'd say, 'Well I've known him all my life since I was about four years old.'

Anyway, in the end he had to come out of hospital, so Margaret had him at home. They turned the front room, it was quite a big house, and she turned what was her front bedroom downstairs into a sort of a place for Dick. He had a single bed there, well the hospital supplied everything, he had a hospital bed, everything, catheters, and she had carers come in three times a day.

Margaret nursed him right up to the end. Vera and I would go over and give Margaret a break. We'd go over and sit in the conservatory with him sometimes of an afternoon like, you know, Vera and I, and he gradually deteriorated. We used to do a bit of shopping for Margaret. If she wanted some shopping when we went to Sainsbury's, we'd get it for her.

I think it was three weeks before Christmas. We came back one Thursday, as we always went to Sainsbury's on a Thursday, called in, and he'd died two minutes before we got there, so we stayed with Margaret until the undertakers come and took the body away. I helped her a lot with, you know. I went with her to the Registrar, she drives but she's too nervous, she's, I told her she must keep her driving up, but she'd only drive to Waitrose, it was the only place she'd drive. Oh, I took her down Buddleigh, her dentist was down Buddleigh, in my car and have the bath-chair in the back and then push it from the car park to Dick and Margaret's dentist.

Dick was a lovely chap. We were both Guardian readers, he was very much a liberal in his outlook and so is Margaret. We didn't used to argue politics but he was quite a knowledge box you know, he knew what he was talking about and he didn't matter if he upset friends or nothing, he stuck to what he believed in. But eventually he died, I think it was a fortnight or three weeks before Christmas and I ran Margaret round the Births and Deaths and done the various things to help.

The funeral was in Exeter Crematorium and I collected his ashes in the end and took them up Salcombe Regis with Margaret and Vera and we had them put in a little grave up there and then Margaret had a wake.

They had a lot of friends in London and they came down. I only found this out since he died; Dick was a Sunday School Teacher and he was in the choir in the church and there were twelve of them in the choir and the twelve of them and their wives met up every year from when he joined the church. They used to go and have a lunch and what not and perhaps have a weekend away, and there are only now, I think Margaret was telling me last week or the week before, there's only four of them left now like, you know.

I talked to Margaret about his death, because I was thinking about myself when I did this shuffling, walking business, I thought have I got the same as Dick?

So I asked her, 'What did Dick die of?'

She said, 'On his death certificate he died of vascular heart disease which affected his walking.'

But he was a lovely chap old Dick was, there was no side of him, he wasn't snooty and that, he was a good, what you'd call a grass-roots bloke, someone like yourself. But he was a friend, well I took him out in the old bath-chair and that.

Margaret was saying that when they done the books it took them over twelve months, he didn't have any time for computers and like that, and Margaret kept on because I had a computer, and she said to him about getting one.

But Dick said, 'Oh, you don't want all that.'

But she bought one after he died, she got a laptop which I'm not impressed with but they wrote the book all by hand and they sat each side of the fire place correcting it. I think she said it took them about twelve months to eighteen months to do it like, you know.

But he came down here from Cobham in Surrey. They had quite a big garden there and I think they were glad to see the back of it. Margaret once worked as an assistant to two research chemists, and then later, after she married she joined the WRVS and worked with the library carrying books to the housebound.

Chapter Twenty One: Bees

Bees

A Life in Sidmouth

Another thing through my meeting Vera was I became interested in bees. The people that Vera lodged with, Mr & Mrs Thomas, well, her brother-in-law was a signal man at Sidmouth Station. His name was Ted Edwards, and one afternoon I went up to see him in the signal box I think this must have been about the end of July, beginning of August.

Anyway, when I got there, Ted had a bucket for a container of some sort and I said, 'What's that there Ted?'

And he replied, 'Honey.'

I asked, 'Where'd you get the honey from?'

And he said, 'From them means over there, from me bees.'

And he had six hives of bees on the side of the railway embankment opposite the signal box.

I mentioned in an earlier chapter that there were bees when I went to school. The Mills brothers and Mr Giles our headmaster at senior school, had two hives of bees under an apple tree in the school allotments and I used to watch them inspecting the bees and that.

Anyway, I asked Ted Edwards, 'Where exactly?'

He said, 'It came from them bees over there!'

And I thought, well, if Ted can get honey, I can get honey. So I churned this over in my mind. My father thought I was mad and so did Vera, 'What do you want to keep bees for?'

But immediately I saw this as a source of supplementing our income in a small way.

So, I set to. I got some books from the library on bee-keeping and I decided I was going to keep bees. I scrounged some timber and I

Bees

made my first bee-hive during the winter evenings before the next season, and finally, I bought my first hive of bees from Ted Edwards. He charged me £4 for them I think, for a colony of bees which consisted of eight frames of combs, a queen and the bees.

I always remember, I never had no transport. I went up to see Ted, he got them all ready, he had some perforated zinc on top of the hive, the container with the bees and combs, and I put them on my handlebars and cycled down Winslade Road, down Lymebourne Lane, across the river, up Sid Lane where I'd secured somewhere to keep them in Sidleigh in Sid Road which at that time was occupied by Major Clegg.

I'd been to see Major Clegg previously, about six months before, when he had a leak in his water service pipe. He had a couple of orchards there and an old tennis court, so I asked him if I could have permission to keep my hive of bees there and he was quite enthused.

'Certainly Mr Counter,' he said, and added, 'My father kept bees when we lived in Hertfordshire.'

So he showed me where I could keep them in one of his orchards and I got the hive all ready in place and I took my colony of bees and put them beside the hive on a couple of bricks, opened the front of the hive and let them fly naturally in and out. And then, the following night, I transferred the combs into my own hive. I always remember I fed them with some sugar-syrup to get the queen to lay more. After all I was only a novice. I didn't know much about it but I'd read quite a bit about bee-keeping.

Eventually they built up to quite a strong hive and they swarmed and they went into the house next door belonging to Mr Blanchard, but he wouldn't let me have them back. Mr Blanchard went and got old Mr Ford, grandfather of the current Fords, on the Alexandria Industrial Estate, to collect the swarm, and Major Clegg rang Mr Blanchard up and told him they were my bees but he wouldn't let me have them.

A Life in Sidmouth

Anyway Major Clegg said, 'Go to Michelmore, Davies and Bellamy and tell them you want the bees back!'

But in the end in didn't reach that stage because I went and saw Mr Ford myself, who lived in Vicarage Road, and I said to him, 'I'm only a beginner, it wasn't much of an advert for a member of the Devon Bee Keepers Association.'

Mr Ford was going to charge me £4 to get the bees back. In the end he relented and I had the bees back for free.

I wasn't satisfied with one hive in the first season, so I made another hive. At the end of the season I had two hives, plus the bees had made me 34lb of honey. I wondered what I was going to do with 34lb of honey. Anyway, I decided to sell it for 1/7d a lb.

All the next winter I used to go up the library and get various books out. I must have had 20 or 30 books from the Exeter library's agricultural section. I was an avid reader of bee books to improve my knowledge. I also used to do dissection of bees and mount them on slides, the sting, the eyes, the legs etc. and cover them with Canadian Balsalm.

In the meantime I was put in touch with Mrs Mole who, eventually I suppose, became my mentor.

Mrs Mole lived in Hillcote in the High Street at Sidford. She was a very talented bee-keeper. In fact, she was a very talented person. Both she and her husband, who had passed away, were members of the magic circle. They'd done conjuring, rag pictures and she was in the W.I. Mrs Mole was into everything and was a very competent bee-keeper.

Through Mrs Mole I joined the Devon Bee Keepers Association and I used to go along to all the meetings and that. On one Saturday in June there was a meeting at Bicton College and I cycled there and met a Mr and Mrs East, who I found out afterwards, had retired to

Bees

Sidmouth from Chesham in Buckinghamshire. It was through these meetings that I became very friendly with Mr and Mrs East.

They used to come down the house and they invited Vera and I and the girls up to their place. They lived in Newlands Road and Mr East had about eight hives of bees. Mr East and I used to sort of help each other. If he wanted any help I would give him a hand, like if he wanted to find any queens or anything. Mr East was a very handy man. His business in Chesham had been in the timber business and in his garage he had a lathe he used to make various parts for his bee-keeping. Anyway, I helped him and he done the same for me.

Over a period of years I expanded and ended up at one time with thirty-nine hives of bees. I had three Apiaries, one in Sid Road at the bottom of Milltown Lane in the orchard. Mrs Mole eventually gave up bee-keeping and I bought her Apiary, she had an Apiary with eight hives out at Sidbury at Ridgeway, Sidbury, and I purchased these from her. She wanted me to have them. She helped me enormously with my knowledge of bee-keeping but eventually I became a better bee keeper than what she was, but Mrs Mole was a lovely person. If she wanted a hand with anything I would give her a hand. She didn't have a car and neither did I.

And I remember on one occasion a Mrs Winkworth who lived at Sidmouth House in Cotmaton Road, she bought two hives of bees. She didn't have much experience but after purchasing them she found they were bad tempered and on this particular occasion she had about three quarters of a hundred-weight of honey on each hive and she went to remove a crop of honey but the bees were so ferocious she had to pack it up and she asked Mrs Mole if she could attempt to get her honey crop off.

Anyway, Mrs Mole asked if I would like to go and give her a hand so we went up there one evening to remove the honey crop.

Good gracious, it was unbelievable! We opened the roof of the hive, smoked them in the front as we usually did, when you open the hive a couple of puffs of smoke in the front and then lifted the roof off to get to the honey and that, and they came out in droves! They were the most ferocious bees Mrs Mole or myself had ever handled. We literally had dozens and dozens of stings on our ankles and legs, and they even got inside our trousers.

Anyway, we had to abandon them in the end. The hives were on the top of a bank and Mrs Mole and I literally rolled down the bank crushing the bees that were stinging us. We had to go back another evening with some slightly mild chloroform. We removed the honey as quick as we could by working together as fast as we could. We removed the honey and I think altogether there was 165lbs of honey in the two hives.

The ferocity of the bees frightened Mrs Winkworth so much she sold them and gave up bee-keeping.

Here's another thing that happened through Mrs Mole. Mrs Mole looked after a gentleman's bees up at Sidbury Hill at Littlefields, a Capt Francis Reynolds Verdon. Anyway Mrs Mole, who was much older than me, she was an elderly lady, was going to give up bee keeping and asked me if I would take on looking after the bees for Capt. Verdon? This I agreed to do, so the last time she went up to Littlefields she took me with her.

Captain Francis Reynolds Verdon was a very, very nice gentleman. He treated me with great respect and that, and always called me Mr Counter. He had been, I found out afterwards, the head of the Montgomeryshire Yeomanry and was the Sheriff of Montgomeryshire in 1930. He had a big estate at Llanerchydol Hall, Welshpool.

Anyway, I agreed to take on the job of looking after his bees. I had no transport, only a bicycle in those days, but Capt. Verdon would either send a taxi to fetch me or he would come himself in his car and take me up to Littlefields.

He was a perfect gentleman. His wife was called Beatrice and he had three daughters but he always treated me with great respect, whenever I went there. It didn't matter who was there, he always invited me in, and if it was a pleasant day, which it usually was, we would go out on the veranda and sit, after I'd finished the bees. I'd have a cup of tea, if I wanted it, or more than likely we would have a glass of beer and Mrs Verdon would have a gin and tonic.

Quite often he would say, 'Bring your wife Mr Counter, she could walk round the garden with B and wander around.'

He had a nice pond there, nice roses, a beautifully kept garden and also a nice tennis court. And I looked after his bees, and even after he died, I still continued to look after them, altogether for twenty-six years.

Another person I met through my bee-keeping, again it might have been through Mrs Mole, was Mr Morrant.

Mr Morrant lived in a flat with his wife at Asherton in Cotmaton Road. The house has since gone and some terraced houses erected in its place by Broseley Homes. The house was right opposite Cheese Lane actually. He was another gentleman, and he and I got on like a house-on-fire. He kept his bees out at 'The Boyd.'

He used to drive a 'Jag,' and he used to take me out if he couldn't find his queens or something. He used to take me out and I'd find his queens and mark them for him. He had a nice shed out there, a hand-lathe (a treddle-lathe), and Mr Morrant was a very keen fisherman and used to tie his own 'flies.'

We used to have days out together. He used to ring me and say, 'Devon Bee Keepers Annual General Meeting Mr Counter.'

He said it was our day out together and we used to go to the Annual General Meeting in the Hatherleigh Laboratories at Exeter University every year and we'd have lunch. He treated me to lunch and tea as a way of thanking me for my help during the year.

A Life in Sidmouth

Mr Morrant also introduced me to fly-fishing. He gave me, well he didn't give me a rod, he sold me a rod. The rod was quite valuable and I had it for many, many years, in fact it was only about four years ago I sold it. He said I could have it but I had to pay him half-a-crown for it, because if you didn't pay for something you didn't value it. That was his sort of philosophy.

I enjoyed a good relationship with Mr Morrant as I did with Capt. Verdon and the family. They always treated me very well, but I nearly blotted my copy-book with Mr Morrant because of something that happened back in the very bad winter we had in 1962-63.

I lost twelve hives of bees at an Apiary I had out at Sidbury in Lincombe Lane. Because of the severe weather the hives were attacked by green woodpeckers who bored holes into the sides, the weakest part where the grooves were that acted as handles, and took the bees and the honey. I couldn't get out to them because in the lane the snow was as high as the hedges. When I did eventually get out there I found that all the hives had been attacked by woodpeckers and one woodpecker was caught up in one of the wires of the frames.

Anyway, the Sidmouth Herald at the time, and Harvey Culverwell the owner of the Sidmouth Herald who I knew very well and used to go prawning with, put a humorous article in the paper, under the headline 'Breaking and Entering at Sidbury.' It reported that I'd lost all these bees and that, and Mr Morrant read the article.

He came down to see me but I was at work. Anyway, he told my wife he wanted to see me so I went and saw him and he offered me a sum of money to buy new hives and re-stock my Apiary.

But I said, 'No thank you, I've always stood on my own feet and I'll build it up again as I had before.'

I didn't want any help and he was upset about this. He said, 'You can have the money for as long as you wanted. If you don't pay it back I'd think none the worse of you. I don't want no interest for it, I just want to help you,' he said, 'You've been a good friend to me.'

Anyway I refused him and he came back to see Vera, my wife again, saying he was upset that Gerald wouldn't take his offer like you know and she said, 'Well that's the way he is Mr Morrant, he's always stood on his own feet!'

So we nearly parted company over this. Poor Mr Morrant got quite upset about this, that I wouldn't accept his help and our friendship nearly finished over it.

So in the end, because he got so upset I said to him, 'Alright.'

So I had the money from him. I put it in the bank, had twelve months interest on it, and I paid it back exactly twelve months after he let me have it. He was very pleased and we parted the best of friends in the end.

All these people I met through bee-keeping and I used to go to all the Bee-keeping Meetings and that.

I met a man called Donald Sims, he was a great Bee Keeper, he was from the North. He moved down to Devon to Trude House near Exeter. He was a great bee keeper, in fact in later years he wrote a book 'Sixty Years with Bees.'

How he came to Devon was he'd done the enquiry for the Oakhampton-Bypass, he was a man that worked for the Ministry and that. But Donald Sims was truly a great bee keeper. I met him at Devon Bee Keepers Meetings.

I took some bees to Dartmoor three or four times as I wanted to specialise in producing 'heather honey.' A friend had let me have his pick-up truck and John Mortimore, who I'd been friends with through prawning and that, his brother was living in Sidmouth at the time, he used to drive the pick-up truck for me. He used to take about eight hives of bees down to Dartmoor. Prior to the first occasion I wrote to

'Brother Adam' the world renowned bee breeder. He was a monk at Buckfast Abbey and travelled the world searching for improved strains of bees, and breeding and crossing them in isolated Apiaries on Dartmoor.

I wrote to Brother Adam because I didn't want to go to Dartmoor and find somewhere to put my hives for the heather and find I was interfering with some of his bee breeding work. So I wrote to him and asked him if he could recommend somewhere to take bees and he recommended a place near Chagford, I think it was Hangershell Rock, I'm not sure. Another place he recommended was near Hexworthy and Fernworthy.

Anyway, eventually I ended up near Fernworthy Reservoir. I wrote to the engineer of the South Devon Water Board requesting if they would let me keep some bees on some ground near Fernworthy Reservoir away from the public, which I was lucky and they did.

But in writing to Brother Adam I asked him if at any time he had any queen bees to sell I'd be interested in purchasing one to improve my stock. He wrote back a very nice letter suggesting where I could go but nothing about the queen bees. But, I think it was the Wednesday after the August Bank Holiday 1957 an envelope came through the post with a queen-cage inside, which is the normal method of sending bees through the post, with a queen bee in, and I used this for mating with my own bees and improving my stock, and they were very, very good. They were good honey-getters, they made nice wax-cappings and that.

Capt. Verdon at this time also wanted to improve his stock so I wrote to a gentleman, who was a dairy farmer in the Tyne Valley, near Newcastle, Colin Weightman, and I purchased two nuclei (small colony of bees) with a queen from him.

They duly arrived by rail and they were very similar to Brother Adam's bees. Brother Adam and Colin Weightman were friends. If Brother Adam went north he always went and visited and stayed with Colin Wightman. I think he had a dairy farm, I think I'm right in saying, in Stocksfield in the Tyne Valley. Colin's bees were also exceptional good honey getters.

After a time Brother Adam started sending some of his breeder queens to Weaver Brothers who were the world's largest queen breeders in Texas, America, but they weren't a patch, I did purchase one of these queens later, but they weren't a patch on the original one I had from Brother Adam or the ones I purchased from Colin Weightman on Capt. Verdon's behalf.

The difference, I think, is that where the climate out in America is more reliable, this is why Brother Adam sent them out there, and they used to re-import them and sell them to bee keepers in this country but they weren't, I don't think they were a patch on the original queens or nuclei that I had from Brother Adam or Colin Wightman. And I also found after a time that when they got crossed with local bees they could become very vicious, and although they produced bees in enormous quantities, they weren't great honey getters I found.

In 1958, I think it was, I showed some honey for the first time at the Sidford Show.

I showed for myself and I showed for Capt. Verdon, using his honey and my own honey and we both won prizes. I ended up bitten by the show bug and I started sending my honey, for quite a few years, I sent honey all over the country to various shows, Birmingham, National Honey Show in London, Royal Cornwall Show, Devon County Show, High Wycombe, National Dairy Show, Radstock, near Midsomer Norton and Hansworth Park. All these were quite big honey shows and over a period of several years, I collected, I think I'm right in saying this, over two hundred and ninety prizes for honey.

Another thing that happened in 1957 was that while working for the Sidmouth Urban District Council, I had an appointment to see the Clerk of the Council one Wednesday morning, and I was sent up to the Clerk's office, which was Mr Pickard. I was called in and Mr Pickard introduced me to this lady that was sat there.

A Life in Sidmouth

'This is Miss Robinson, she's from the BBC Gerald, '

Her name was Phyllis Robinson I believe, and Mr Pickard said to her, 'This is Gerald, the bee keeper.'

And Mr Pickard turned to me and said, 'Miss Robinson represents the BBC.'

Miss Robinson said, 'I produce the programme 'Down Your Way' with Franklin Engelmann,' and went on, 'Would you be interested? We'd like Mr Engelmann to interview you on bee-keeping?'

So arrangements were made and at one o'clock I went to my Apiary in Sid Road and met Mr Engelmann with the BBC's technical people with all the recording instruments. Miss Robinson introduced me to Mr Engelmann and we shook hands, he was a very nice man. I thought he was a perfect gentleman.

He said, 'Can we wander down amongst your bee hives?'

I said, 'Are you nervous about getting stung?'

'No, I don't think so,' he said.

And we wandered amongst the bees for about half an hour. He me asked questions, we discussed this and various things about bee-keeping and then he said, 'Do you think you're ready now, could you do the interview?'

So I said, 'Yes I think so.'

So we went up the driveway of Sidleigh where the bees were and he introduced me as, 'I've got a gentleman, not with a bee in his bonnet but a bee on his tie,' because I had a brooch on my tie of a queen bee. And he asked me various questions about bee-keeping, queen rearing, honey production, most aspects of bee-keeping. Some that were more technical than others and would be uninteresting to the general public.

Bees

Anyway the interview took about half an hour I suppose and at the end he said, 'At the end of Down Your Way each participant had a choice of music,' so he said, 'I expect you'll want Rimsky-Korsakov's 'Flight of the Bumble-Bee' would you?'

And I replied, 'No, what I would like is the 'Toreador Song' from Bizet's Carmen,' which they duly played when they broadcast the programme one Sunday afternoon at quarter past five.

There were other Sidmouthians on the programme apart from myself. Sid Spiller from Burscombe Farm spoke on Cider-making, Bill Cranaford spoke on coach tours (Dagwothys), Miss Nan Barnard spoke about Honiton Lace Making (she lived in Banwell House in Old Fore Street opposite the National Trust shop) and Mr Dingwell spoke on Sidmouth Architecture and R W Sampson the well-known Sidmouth Architect.

The programme came out in July 1957 but unfortunately BBC Bristol never retained any of the old tapes, only the later ones that Brian Johnstone, the cricket chap, did when he took over from Franklin Engelmann. Franklin Engelmann was a stockbroker apparently. He gave that career up and got a job with the BBC.

But my bee-keeping brought me into contact with many various people of all walks of life. One of the most important things that happened through my dealings with bees was that I became a bit of a social service for in the town was collecting swarms. The police used to ring up and say there was a swarm at so-and-so, or else the Council would ring up and say there is a swarm and could I go and collect it and that which I always did.

One went off with a straw skep which is a straw basket, the method was that you'd put the skep underneath the swarm, if it was easy to get at, and give the branch that the swarm had settled on a sharp shake with your fist or something and the whole lot dropped down en-masse into the skep and you had a white sheet on the ground, put the skep on the white sheet, turn it upside down and put a stone under one edge so the bees could go in and out and usually you were lucky, I never had much trouble, if you got the queen in they would all troop in, the bees would,

To watch a swarm of bees when they go into a hive or you put them in the skep is quite amazing. They've got a scent gland at the end of their abdomen called the Nasanov (or Nassanoff) gland, named after the Russian anatomist who first described it. They would give off a scent and the bees would, you'd see the bees standing, fanning, this scent, calling the other bees in, and by the end of the day, I would leave them there till late evening, and then go and collect them. I would then turn them upside down, lay a sheet over them, tie a piece of string all the way round, take them to one of my Apiaries and put them in an empty hive. You'd put a board down the front of the empty hive, turn the skep upside down, give it a thump, and you'd have a white cloth over the board and they'd all march up in the entrance of the hive. I used to watch the, I used to have a goose wing or something to brush them in, and you'd see the old queen going into the hive and once she'd gone in the hive you'd see them trooping in like an army.

I remember the Police got onto me one day about some bees causing a nuisance at 'Camden' in Elysian Fields.

The sergeant rang me, 'Here Gerald,' he said, 'We're having trouble with Brigadier Widmore's wife, she's got a swarm of bees up in her chimney and she keeps ringing us up two or three times a day. Can you do something about it?'

So I said, 'Yeah, all right then, where are they?'

'In the chimney!' he said.

'Oh God, they're a damn nuisance in the chimney,' I replied.

Over the years I only did about four or five swarms that were in the chimney.

Bees

Anyway I went up and saw Brigadier Widmore's widow, a short but polite lady, and I said 'What's the trouble madam? I'm Gerald Counter. I've come about your bees. The Police asked me to see you.'

'Oh yes,' she said, 'they're up there!'

So, we went out on the lawn and looked up to the chimneys and I couldn't see no bees. To me there was no sign of any bees.

Eventually I said, 'I can't see no bees madam. I don't think they are in your chimney.'

"Oh I'm sure they are," she said.

Anyway I said, 'Well, maybe, but I can't see any at the moment.'

So I went home and I rang the Police Station and I said, 'There ain't no bees up there Sargeant,' I said.

Anyway, two or three days later I met him down the town.

'Here,' he said, 'can't you do anything about those damn bees, she rings up every day. Isn't there nothing you can do?'

'Yeah, all right Sargeant,' I said, 'I'll see what I can do for you.'

So I went back up to Camden and knocked on the door.

Mrs Widmore came out and I said, 'Can we look at which chimney you think . . .? Ah yes madam,' I said, 'there are some bees up there.'

She said, 'I can hear them in my bedroom!'

So I went up into her bedroom which had a gas fire in it, and I said, 'Alright leave it with me, I'll deal with them.' I said, 'I'll leave it till a dull day.'

A Life in Sidmouth

So a dull day came and back I went. I got a sack with a load of newspapers, some old dried up honeycomb that I had and I put it in the sack and took some tools with me because I told her I had to take the gas fire out.

I went up to the bedroom. I locked the door, and sat on the bed for a few minutes.

Mrs Widmore called out, 'Can I come in?'

I replied, 'No madam, I wouldn't want you to get stung!'

'Well what about yourself then Mr Counter?'

I said, 'I'm immune to it madam,' I said. 'Don't worry about that!'

So I got my tools that I took with me and banged them together and banged the pipe that was going to the gas fire and what-not and I went back and sat on the bed for about five or ten minutes.

Mrs Widmore called out again, 'You alright in there!'

'Yes I'm alright madam,' I said, 'give me another ten minutes and I'll be out!'

'Have you done it?' she asked

'Yes I think I have,' I said.

She replied, 'I'll be downstairs.'

So I waited another ten minutes, quarter of an hour, and then came out. I went downstairs and there she was sat in the lounge.

'Have you been successful?' she asked.

I said, 'Yes madam.'

Bees

I then opened my sack and took out a handful of the contents and showed her some parts of the honeycomb and a few old dead bees I'd put in there.

'Oh!' she said, 'Thank you so much, thank you so much,' she said, 'It's been worrying me for a long time,' she said.

'Yes, so I understand from the Police madam,' I said.

She asked, 'What do I owe you?'

I said, 'Nothing madam, that's all right, no charge,' I said.

'Would you like a drink with me?' she asked.

I said, '"That would be very nice.'

'What would you like? Would you like a whisky?' she said.

'No, I . . '

'Would you like a beer?'

So I had a beer with her, I think it was a bottle of Bass, I'm not sure but it gave me a headache.

Then she said, 'What about a sherry before you go?'

So she gave me a sherry before I went, I think it was a Croft's Original, and we parted the best of friends. She was happy the bees had gone.

I'd told a filthy lie, and that, but the Police were happy as sand-boys that I'd got her off their back.

That's absolutely true. If Sgt. Douggie Holsgrove was still living he'd confirm that.

A Life in Sidmouth

'Cor, thank God for that Gerald,' he said. 'Blooming nuisance!' he used to say.

I found that bees always seemed to fascinate people, if you mentioned you were a bee keeper people always wanted you to explain about their natural life, one thing or another.

For instance, it's estimated that a pound (lb) of honey represents about 45,000 flights out and back for bees to collect a lb of honey. When they collect nectar from the plants it's got about 70% water content. A bee has two stomachs, a true stomach and a honey stomach in which the substance is stored, and when they go back to the hive, they regurgitate the honey, put it in the cells and then they fan, they create an airflow that dries off the excess moisture until it becomes pure honey.

At one time I was asked to do some talks on bee-keeping and I done, I suppose, all together about sixteen or seventeen talks locally to various organisations and it always fascinated them.

Towards the end I found out the best way to introduce the subject or to get the best out of people to ask questions was to ask them to start off by asking me questions about what they wanted to know about bees.

I used to say, 'I want to tell you what you want to know about bees, so you start by asking me questions!'

And from there I could develop a reasonable dialogue about bee-keeping. I went to Honiton to the 'Toc H,' which was a charity organisation established during WWI for people in the forces and that. You could go there and have a cup of coffee. A also did the Rotary Club once, the Young Wives and the Methodist Women's Guild.

I really enjoyed my bee-keeping and I had no trouble disposing of my honey crop. It was hard work sometimes in summer months but I got over it, I done everything myself and then for several years I put

Bees

on a display at the Sidford & Salcombe Regis Horticultural Society. I used to have a stand there with honey, honey and marmalade, honey fudge, furniture cream.

I used to take a glass observation-eye for people to look at with a queen marked. It was about 15" wide and 18" tall with glass sides, a wooden frame with glass sides and I used to put in a queen, two combs of bees and honey and pollen. I had it clamped to my stand and people were fascinated by it, you know, and I met numerous people, people I met that became friends for life through bee-keeping.

I used to have people call at the house. I met some Americans one day who came to the house to see me. People, through my 'showing' at various shows, people who came to Sidmouth on holiday would call in, knock at the door in Mill Street and ask if I was in, and was I the gentleman that showed honey and that and I'd invite them in. On several occasions I had one chap who used to come down from the Wirral near Chester and he used to, he stayed till gone midnight on a couple of nights just talking bees and bee-keeping.

Of course, about this time, I came into bee-keeping, I think, at the right time. I did think at one time that I would be interested in making a living from bees but it never came to that. But at that time, one of the best adverts for English honey was Russian born Dr Barbara Moore when she used to walk in the early 1960s. She walked from John o' Groats to Land's End in 23 days. She was a great honey eater and vegetarian. She was a great advert for English honey.

When I look back now I think the first pots of honey I sold for 1/7 per lb and now I think English honey fetches £5.00, I've seen it £6.00 in some places.

I don't know if we ever suffered from an over production of English honey but when I look back I think one of the problems today, bees have become more prone to disease and that. In the last twenty years we've been troubled with Varroa mite which is a parasite that feeds of adult bee body fluids.

A Life in Sidmouth

I think it was 1914 when most of the bees in the country were wiped out by what is known as Acarine disease. This was a mite that used to invade the trachea, which is the breathing tubes of the bee and choked them up, and practically all the bees in the country were wiped out and there was quite a concern and bees were imported from the continent to restock our hives in this country.

Most people look on bees as producers of honey but their prime purpose of bees is really in pollination and the production of fruit. Their economic value to the country is tremendous.

I really enjoyed my bee-keeping and when I look back I had a very good time with them. I had my ups and downs but on the whole I wouldn't have given up my bees for anything. Well, I kept them in the end for sixty-one years, and I done it all myself, I never had any help from, well, a friend of mine John Hawkins used to help me over two or three years over extracting the honey.

That's the hardest time is when you take off, you remove your crop of honey, bring it back and you extract the honey in a machine by centrifugal force and from there it goes in what is known as a settling tank which brings all the froth and that to the top and from there it's allowed to settle.

My system was that it's alright if you've got a few hives but my system was, some people like clear honey, some people like the thick honey, my method was to extract the honey and I stored it in 28lb tins and over a period of two or three months. It would go solid and then I used to warm it back in a heating cabinet and some I would bottle as clear honey and the other was bottled when reset, so that you could take it from the jar and spread it easily on one's toast or bread and butter.

My wife Vera also used to make honey cake, in fact she showed honey cake in the Exeter Show once and she took some prizes which she was quite 'chuffed' about.

Bees

One year, I think it was around 1968-70, I can't remember the year, but one year I had a very heavy crop and I couldn't handle it at home and Sir Charles Cave let me have his old Ridgeway Dairy that he had. I cleaned it out and decorated it and extracted most of my honey there which was opposite old Ridgeway Farm, I used the dairy that used to belong to Ridgeway Farm. The dairy wasn't in use and I asked Sir Charles if I could rent it from him which he kindly agreed to do and I used that as my extracting place and the honey was all extracted, and strained and put in 28lb tins. It was too much to handle at home.

Some of my most enjoyable hours were spent on Sunday morning going up to the bees in my Apiaries and cleaning them up in the winter. One of the, what I always thought were the benefits of bee-keeping was that it was, from April until the end of September, a very busy time but the winter period was quiet and one had a period of rest from bee-keeping although many a Sunday morning I would go up after a storm to see if the roofs were all intact and there weren't no damage.

One of the worst disasters that happened was when we had the Sidbury whirlwind on 7 January 1974. I had eleven hives at my Apiary on Rideway Farm and I lost them all bar one. I also had a six by six shed on the site that was full of equipment and I lost all that too.

The whirlwind wrapped television aerials around chimneys and whole chimneys were moved on the structure of the roofs. There were about eight trees in Lincombe Lane and it was just as if a giant had walked up through the lane and caught hold of these trees and twisted them around in his hand as if they were daisies.

John Mortimore, my friend, and I went up the following Sunday morning and we walked for miles through the fields looking for the equipment. All we found was a saw which was about three foot long and all we saw was the handle sticking up in the field.

In the shed I had about fifteen queen excluders (they stop the queens going up into the honey) which were sheets of perforated zinc 18⅛" by 18⅛" square by about a sixteenth of an inch in thickness and we found about five of these within a radius of about a mile and they were exactly like a tennis ball. I could never understand it. They were flat, 18⅛" by 18⅛" square and when we found them they were about the size of a tennis ball, all symmetrical, with the force of the whirlwind that got it.

I never found the shed. I looked. I travelled for miles.

I saw my friend Mr Barber, who was the Superintendent at the Norman Lockyer Observatory, and told him about all this and he said, 'They're most likely still in orbit!'

That's what he told me. I had a whole shed full of equipment, six foot by six foot, and there was nothing there. It was as if it had been ripped away by a giant. There was a massive oak tree on the edge and all there was about twelve feet of the trunk and most of the branches tore off, in fact I think you can still see some of the remnants of the storm up through the lane. It was unbelievable. There was slates tore off the roofs.

One local villager said it happened about half past four in the morning and it was the experience of the noise of an express train passing through the village. I think the Sidmouth Herald carried a whole page about it for the early edition. The people who lived at Cotford Bridge, I can't remember their names of hand, they had five apple trees that they planted several years previous, and they had a 'Crittall' greenhouse which disappeared just like my shed. They never found it, it just went, it disappeared.

The whirlwind, as far as one could ascertain was about fifty yards wide and it just tore off through the village in the early hours of, I think, it was a Monday morning. It's a good job no one was out walking around then because I'm sure they'd have been killed.

Dick Clay's cottage, which was a thatched cottage next up from Ridgeway Farm, the chimney on it was well built. It was a very old cottage but the chimney was made from stone and that one was moved about six yards along the roof. Next to Ridgeway Farm, the lady that lived in there was keen on horses and she had an old cast iron bath, which I found when I went to my Apiary the next morning after the whirlwind. It had been carried somewhere in the region of about five hundred yards and it was implanted in the end of my Apiary half down in the ground.

Never seen anything like it, never to this day, I'd never of believed it. There were trees uprooted.

Ridgeway Apiary, what with the woodpeckers and the whirlwind seemed to be, I began to believe it was, ill-fated. Then on one occasion, I think it was 1974, I was going through my bees and I thought I'd found in one colony American foulbrood (AFB) which is a disease of the bee brood and a notifiable disease to the Ministry of Agriculture.

So I rang the appropriate people, I sent off a comb to Rothamsted in Sussex to confirm it, that's where the bee headquarters was in those days, the Ministry of Agriculture, and they confirmed that it was American foulbrood.

So I got a Mr Lancaster, who came from Tavistock, whom I had previously met on other occasions, and he came and confirmed it.

The only thing to do is to burn the hive and all the combs. The procedure is to dig a pit about three or four feet deep, you kill the bees off by closing the entrance and putting a drop of petrol on a cloth on the top and it kills them instantaneously and then you put all the combs into the pit and you burn the lot. But what I done as a precautionary measure, I only had it in one hive, but as a precautionary measure I destroyed six other hives that I had in the Apiary and burnt all those as well and I never kept no bees in those hives for twelve months as a precautionary measure. And the hives were all burnt and singed inside with a blow-lamp.

I didn't have to destroy the other hives but I done it as a precautionary measure but it paid off because I never had a return of the disease for the rest of my bee-keeping career. The Ministry chap said there was no need to go to that trouble but I said as a precautionary measure I didn't want to be bothered with it in the future because it can recur.

So I took the decision to destroy the rest of the colonies and then I never kept any bees there for twelve months and I consider that was the best measure I took and after twelve months I re-stocked the Apiary from my other Apiaries I had at Sid Road and Trow Hill. That was the only time that I experienced any of the brood diseases and that.

I went to the National Honey Show one year, I think it was 1958, at Conway Hall in London and I was introduced to two of the National Judges.

I wanted to enquire about one or two things and they said to me, 'Where do you come from?'

And I said, 'Sidmouth.'

And I was very proud when they both turned round and said, 'You come from the cleanest seaside place in England and you've also got one of the most respected Town Clerks in the country.'

Of course, they were referring to the late Mr R Pickard. And I was rather proud to have been at the National Honey Show to be told that about my home town.

Finally, when I look back, I had sixty-one years of bee-keeping and I enjoyed every minute of it. It was hard work in a good season getting the honey crop off, taking it home, extracting it, but I enjoyed every minute.

Bees

Chapter Twenty Two: M.N.D.

M.N.D.

A Life in Sidmouth

See, I've thought a lot about this Motor Neurone Disease. When I think about it, four or five years ago, when we was shopping in Sainsbury's for about eight weeks, I had a high sensation in my shin-bones, mostly in my left leg, as if there was water rushing and my skin felt tight on my legs afterwards and it was most uncomfortable.

I might have mentioned it to you when we used to natter away on a Monday. But I've thought about this, I put it down to shopping in Supermarkets when you shuffle around instead of walking and you don't circulate the blood properly. I thought a lot about this.

And then about twelve months after that started I had this terrific pain in my left leg and I went and saw Dr Slot. He was on holiday and I saw Dr Fung.

He said, 'You'll have to come up this afternoon and have an injection.'

It was a Thursday and I had to go again on Friday morning and have another injection, and he said, 'I'm going to send you to Honiton this afternoon to have a digital scan on your leg.'

And I went to Honiton. Olwen took me up, and saw Dr Silver, a happy go-lucky chap.

I was worried about clotted blood, and he said, 'There are no clots of blood, none at all, and there's no need to come on Saturday or Sunday.' This was because they were also talking about me going on Saturday and Sunday for more injections because they were concerned about this terrific pain I had. But the pain subsided and I went back to Dr Slot a week later, he had come back from holiday, and everything was alright.

Then I had another pain one day in this left leg and my knees started giving me trouble. That was when they sent me for an x-ray and I was referred to physiotherapy. I started physiotherapy a fortnight before Christmas. I done my usual exercises and then went back after the Christmas break to finish another four weeks treatment.

It was the following April, 2012, the 19th I think it was, I'm almost positive, when I was coming out of the garden shed and fell backwards. I've thought of all of this since. That was the beginning of my falls. I didn't fall again for another four or five months. I remember I was just inside the shed and as I went down I grabbed the sides of the shed. I gripped the sides as I came out backwards and I was worried I'd get splinters in my hands but I didn't get any. I was sliding, my hands slid down and I went down 'bang' on the ground outside my shed, but I managed to retrieve myself, went indoors, and I told Vera I'd fallen out of the shed. I thought nothing of it.

And I never thought, even then, of my, I never think I'm 86, I still think I'm about 21 or, I never think of an age at all, I still feel as well as when I did when I was back then. I mean physically and mentally I feel still young, except I've got these blasted hands now and I can't move me legs, I don't feel anything wrong with me at all.

Because after I started these falls Dr Slot sent me back to physiotherapy again. Then after that I told the physiotherapist I don't seem to be getting anywhere.

I said, 'What about this knee, why can't I bend my knee?'

So she referred me to Exmouth Hospital.

This chap, he didn't say anything about Motor Neurone, he said, 'It could be your foot plantar, your balance is out!'

I began to think it was something to do with my ears.

He said, 'Stand upright and walk towards me.'

I did this and then I walked backwards.

A Life in Sidmouth

He said, 'You've got a balance problem!'

Of course, after I saw him and I continued the physiotherapy for another six weeks but then I started falling regularly and somehow I always fell backwards. The only time I fell forwards was when I tripped on the mat in Vinnicombe's one Saturday morning. I was going to take Vera into The Chattery for lunch and I went in to get some bread and caught me toe on the mat inside the door and I fell full frontal then. After every 'falling' episode I could always get up, it's still a mystery to me, the fact that at 85 I could still get up.

It was after, I suppose, when I went into hospital, and came back to Sidmouth the first time. The physiotherapist at Sidmouth had me walking, I was up and down in the wards, I went down the Ham on me own a couple of times but I felt I wasn't getting anywhere. Then when they said to me in Sidmouth Hospital for a fortnight you can go home now, I thought, I tried my best to get around, but I began to get doubts in my mind I was going to get anywhere. I thought it was getting most difficult to get out of the chair. I couldn't put my hands on the chair and raise my elbows.

I fell backwards in the front room one day and I caught my chin on the mantelpiece as I went down. I managed to get up but I had to manipulate myself into a position to get my right leg against the settee to get the leverage to get up as I had no power in my left leg.

Of course then I went to see Dr Lars-Ola Tostie, at the Sidmouth Chiropractic Centre in Arcot Road.

Lars said, 'You've got a balance problem,' and added, 'I can't do anything for you.'

He was quite honest about it. Lars, who was due to leave the Centre also said that the new chiropractor, Luke (Dr Luke Hickling MChiro D.C.), may be able to help with my shoulder problem.

I began to get worried too when I used to come over to you (*Julian King*) because you eventually came and fetched me in the car and I used to have to lift my leg in over the door opening. Of course, when I fell down the last time they came and took me in and I saw the consultant neurologist (Mr J Gormley) whom I had, coincidentally, been referred to three weeks previously by Dr Slot at the Sidmouth Health Centre. On my previous meeting Mr Gormley did some tests, including some for balance, but never mentioned MND. This time he told me he would arrange a spinal scan, which I subsequently had but they didn't find anything.

I've digressed a little, to get back to my last fall; my knee gave out at home at the top of the stairs one Sunday morning when the carer was with me. This was two Sundays before last Christmas. See, even then, I was determined I'd get up. I'd shaved myself before the carer came, I'd partly washed myself, and she helped me dress. This time I couldn't get up and the paramedics were called to help and they took me to the Accident and Emergency Centre at Wonford Hospital in Exeter. I still think it's amazing that when I fell I never broke a bone. I fell in Sainsbury's three times, once against a supermarket trolley.

So I said to Mr Gormley, 'I'm not a young man, I said, be honest with me, I've thought about it several, several times. Tell me straight, what have I got?'

Before he could say it, I said, 'Is it Motor Neurone?'

And Mr Gormley replied, 'I'm afraid it is Gerald, but we'll have to do some tests first to confirm it.'

Of course, that's why I had to wait 'til after Christmas. But I'd thought, when I look at my arms, my arms above my elbows, it's just like all skinny flesh, there's no muscle there at all.

I went to see this chap, he was from Iraq, who did the tests with electrical equipment at Wonford Hospital in Exeter. I had so much faith that something would rectify itself because, but it didn't, no I'm not saying I'm devoid of faith, but even them mornings I could tell the difference this morning (10 May 2013) because she came in to take me blood about 6 o'clock, I usually wake about half past six, and I stretch me legs, my ankles and toes forwards and I pull them backwards towards me and then I arch me back about seven times as much as I can and I still had faith sometimes but I never win but I still sometimes think when I get this jumping down my leg when I'm in bed or laying down in the afternoon, there must be life there somewhere but it aint gonna be so I don't think!

I can still feel the nerve endings in the bottom of my feet. The nurse touched the underside of my foot this morning (15 May 2013) and it tickled and I laughed. Some mornings I wake up and my fingers are as straight as a die. But I haven't given up on it all together but I don't want to go on like this for three or four years like, you know. I've never been a pessimist, always an optimist.

I asked Mr Gormley, 'How long I got like you know, be frank with me,' I said, 'come on.'

And he told me, 'I'll give you eighteen months Gerald.'

I told him, 'I'm not afraid of dying.'

Well, naturally, I suppose, Vera, Susan and Olwen are more upset.

There's no pain with the disease, there's no pains in my stomach or anywhere apart from my shoulder. It's so frustrating; I still think I'm so young. I must admit the staff here at Holmesley Nursing Home are very good. They, if my right shoulder was better than what it is I'd be better than I am, I mean 50%, 100%, of any pain I got, comes from my shoulder. They twist me around, they had me on the bed this morning, they wound my legs around to roll me over and that. The nurse that done me blood this morning, she took out, she had eight goes at me like, I've never met anyone like you she said, you're brilliant she said. I said well it's only because I've had bee stings otherwise I wouldn't like to have it nine times or eight times sticking needles in and trying to get the blood out. She was more frustrated than what I was. I said, go on, have another go. No she said, I've had eight goes, I'm not punishing you anymore. You haven't hurt me at all I said.

It might sound terrible to some people, I have accepted it, this is my lot like you know, and I'm going to have to live with 'till the end. There's no cure for it, there's no answer to it and that. At least, I've been told that's the facts so far, that's the most frustrating thing about it, if I feel ill, which I don't feel ill, even now, but I just can't get over there and walk over there, if I could only get over there and open the drawer and get a pen out of there, if I want something, I can't. I've got two plastic containers there at the back of the bed there, I want to put my DVDs in them just to tidy up the top there, if I could only walk over there and do it myself but I can't.

I did say to Mr Gormley last week (W/C Mon 29 April 2013) when I was there, 'Do you think I could try and walk?'

'No,' he said, 'don't go doing that because the state you're in you're likely to fall down and breaks something bad next time. You can't afford to do that Gerald,' he said.

I see Vera walking there but I can't get out of this blooming chair. It's physcological to me, as well as physical, because I just can't do it and I've always been so active like, you know.

Before I go to bed at nights, I don't have any trouble, I sleep all night like a log, I think about my apiaries that I had up at Sidbury and the system I had for doing my 'queens,' I think of that sort of thing and I do go back to when we (*Gerald and Julian King*) first met, and I get more upset, I wanted it to go on forever (*becomes emotionally upset*) ....

Chapter Twenty Three: Looking Back

Looking Back

A Life in Sidmouth

When I look back I've had a wonderful life with a wonderful wife. I've never hankered after wealth. I've led a simple life, near to nature, and I always remember when I went to work and started on the 'Water,' and I had to deal with the public all the time, I always bore in mind that, it don't matter who you're dealing with, but everybody's got feelings. And it's essential if you're dealing with the public that you remember that. It don't matter if it's the lord in his mansion or the chap in his council house, we've all got feelings, and always remember that.

My father came from the country, we had allotments and I wouldn't have changed what I've done one iota. When I look back I'm saddened that Sidmouth is changing but you can't stop progress; whether you can call it progress I don't know. But the thing I miss most about Sidmouth is that a lot of the old characters have disappeared, people like George Collins, Taggie Salter, Georgie Beer, they were all characters in their own right. I've enjoyed every day of my life. I've had my ups and downs, as everyone has ups and downs, but I like to look back and think, the way I lived my life, and I was proud of the town I was born in, and I think I can say when I look back I never done anyone a bad turn.

I still look back at memories as a child when I used to go up with my father after rugby to do the fires at the big house at Cotmaton, and father and I would walk back down through Seafield Road together, then Coburg Road and he always took me in Old Fore Street to Miss Bolt's home made sweet shop, Freeths.

I still remember that to this day.

Miss Bolt used to make all her own sweets and they were all on cake-stands in the window on doilies. Two pennyworth of humbugs my dad used to get me. They were covered with lovely soft sugar and nice and minty. My father was a very kind man.

Vera always said that my father was twice the man I am. She always said that, she worshipped him. He worshipped my two daughters Susan and Olwen but he always said, 'You must always do what your mam and dad tells you!'

Looking Back

One thing I fear, I do worry about today, is that whether young people, I don't know whether I should put this in or no but I do feel this, whether we've lost the work-ethic. For instance, looking back on my life story, I went mushrooming, I went prawning, I kept bees. If you wanted to earn money the only way to do it was to go out and do something. I used to get 2/6d a dozen for big prawns and 1/3d a lb for my mushrooms.

We was never idol as youngsters. On winter evenings we'd be down the Ham playing around with a soccer or rugby ball and other games that all boys played like tag-a-white-tail, tibbet, truth or dare, hopscotch and hide and seek. In the summer we'd be down 'Red-Wall' catching eels. I just like to be able to look back and think, reminiscing away, you've got to remember all the herrings that were caught by the boats of Sidmouth and that, and I can remember from the Bridge by the Ford over as far as 'The Flagstaff' barrels of herrings covered with hessian tops secured with wooden hoops.

Sam Harris, my mother's cousin told us that they used to get 1/2d a stone for the herrings and by the time they'd paid the carrier to take them to Billingsgate Fish Market the fishermen ended up with 2d a stone. Fishermen had a rough time in those days, they might have been miserable but they had something to be miserable about. Times were hard but to me they always stuck together. I can still think of 'Dappy Pinn' the blind-man coming down through the town and 'Tink Harris' and his son Jackie with barrels of fish for sale and Jackie shouting, "Fish-Ah! Fish-Ah! Fish-Ah!" (fresh fish!).

I always remember Jackie Harris saw a scarf in Madam Livesley's shop down town, where Monday's Child is today opposite Tastes ice-cream parlour. Madam Livesley, she came down from London, was a very sophisticated lady, a little short lady and very smart. I bought an Aquascutum jacket in there for Vera once and she wouldn't change it.

I said, 'What if I want to change it, I want it for Christmas?'

'Oh,' she said, 'we don't take second hand clothes back!'

A Life in Sidmouth

'What do you mean second hand clothes? I said

Madam Livesley was ever so short, she wore little booties.

Anyway Vera and I had gone for a walk one night and we came down through Old Fore Street and Jackie Harris, who used to live next door to our house, said, 'Cor, bugger me Gerald,' he said, 'come over here and see this! What the hell do you make of this?' he said. 'Got a bloody scarf in here,' he said, '£14.00! What the hell! Do they think there's money here?'

That's what he was like. He was the one, Jackie Harris and Waller Pike, he worked for the council, he was a road sweeper, what they call a bit of a blow-hard.

Anyway, I remember once we went to Twickenham, to the rugby, and we had a coach. Phil Duffet, the landlord of the Black Horse, organised it. And we went from Sidmouth on a coach to Exeter, and then we had a train from Exeter to London. We went on to Twickenham, went to the match, England v Wales, then we came out and went back to Victoria Street in London where the Black & White Minstrels used to be. Wasn't it down from there they had the headquarters of Whitbreads Brewery?

Well we all went down there, a whole crowd of us went to a pub there and Jackie Harris and Waller Pike, this is a true story, they went in there and we went in and Jackie was all shouting and so was Waller Pike, you could hear them a mile away.

Anyway we came out, I don't know if we got a trolly (bus) or not, anyway we got back to Waterloo and came down on what they used to call the mail train or paper train, Saturday night like, bringing the papers down, and we got into Exeter, got on the coach, everybody piled in, a good day out.

And then somebody said, 'Where's Waller and Jackie Harris to?'

Looking Back

Jackie Harris and Waller Pike had gone to the toilet when we was coming out of the pub and they'd come out the wrong entrance and they missed us and they were stuck up there. And this was supposed to be true.

Anyway they went to a Police Station and they said, 'We men of Devon where Drake came from!' They demanded bed and breakfast and asked the Station Officer, 'Have you never heard of Drake or Raleigh?'

Anyway they stayed in the Police Station all night but they had to come back. It was an excursion and I believe it was £2.30 or something, but they had to pay full fare coming back. I believe it was Phil Duffet and Pat his wife had to go round and tell Waller Pike's wife and Jackie's Mrs. that they wouldn't be home because they didn't come home with the rest of us. They never let them out of Sidmouth again!

I think, looking back, there was more community spirit back in those days than what we've got today. There's still lots of community spirit today but I'm think about the old locals, 'Scrummer', people don't talk about Scrummer, Ern Hayman, Dodger, he was a miserable old sod (*Gerald laughs to himself*), Whopee-Nela Russell, who remembers these people today?

Looking back, one hears so much today about the community and the community spirit and that, but one must remember that today many of the properties are holiday homes, from the Mill bridge and the Ford, where I was born nearby, down to the swimming pool there are about seventy-two holiday cottages, which includes Holmdale, York Street, East Street, Russell Street, Mill Street and places like that.

The old families have all disappeared and the houses have been sold for holiday homes, these people are only here today and gone tomorrow. I don't know what the answer to it is. This is a result of economic affluence as far as I'm concerned anyway, and one cannot stop progress, if this is progress.

I mean, today there's no need, as I said in my earlier writings, there's no need for a 'coal-club' today, or a 'clothing-club' run by the likes of Miss Cowan. She was a Scottish lady who lived in St Kilda on Salcombe Hill.

People are more affluent. In the old days people had linoleum on the floor, today everyone has fitted carpets, and affluence does create its own problems in communities. I've only recently heard they've been talking about a new estate with gated-entrances. To me this isn't the Sidmouth I grew up in.

The fishing community, where there were prominent fishermen years ago, the Harris's, the Woolleys, Hayman Salter, 'Scrummer,' 'Dodger' and the likes, they all had their drifters with their red sails, about eight of them, and went off herring drifting and mackerel fishing, but that's all gone today, the only fishing community that's left today are more or less amateurs compared to the old fishermen. The Harris family consisted of Reg and Cecil, Roy, Tom, 'Tink,' 'Tussie', all with their own sons who went fishing, eg: Tussie Harris's's sons were Roy, Bill, Jimmy and Sid. Today our fishermen are more or less amateurs, they've got second jobs.

Sidmouth has changed so much to me but finally I'd like to say there's nowhere else I wanted to live in. I'm proud of my town and never wished to live anywhere else. Unfortunately, in writing this, I haven't got much longer to go. I've been diagnosed with Motor Neurone Disease (MND) so the 'Play-of-Sidmouth' as far as I'm concerned is coming to a close, but I've enjoyed every minute of living in this town.

I've had a good life and what more could I ask?